Attaining the 2030 Sustainable Development Goal of Good Health and Well-Being

FAMILY BUSINESSES ON A MISSION

Queensland, Australia

Series Editors:

Naomi Birdthistle
Rob Hales

The Family Businesses on Mission series examines how the United Nations Sustainable Development Goals (UN SDGs) can be applied in family businesses around the world, providing insights into cultural and societal differences and displaying innovative approaches to complex environmental and societal issues.

Other Titles in This Series

Attaining the 2030 Sustainable Development Goal of Good Health and Well-Being

EDITED BY

NAOMI BIRDTHISTLE

Griffith University, Australia

AND

ROB HALES

Griffith University, Australia

United Kingdom – North America – Japan – India – Malaysia – China

Emerald Publishing Limited
Emerald Publishing, Floor 5, Northspring, 21-23 Wellington Street, Leeds LS1 4DL

First edition 2024

Editorial matter and selection © 2024 Naomi Birdthistle and Rob Hales.
Individual chapters © 2024 The Authors.
Published by Emerald Publishing Limited.

 Open Access

The ebook edition of this title is Open Access and is freely available to read online.

British Library Cataloguing in Publication Data
A catalogue record for this book is available from the British Library

ISBN: 978-1-80455-212-4 (Print)
ISBN: 978-1-80455-209-4 (Online)
ISBN: 978-1-80455-211-7 (Epub)

Printed and bound by CPI Group (UK) Ltd, Croydon, CR0 4YY

INVESTOR IN PEOPLE

Contents

List of Figures

List of Tables

About the Editors

Professor Naomi Birdthistle has entrepreneurship and family business running through her veins. She tried to work in her family business when she was four but was told she was too small. She came back year after year asking to work and eventually her grandmother capitulated and left her work in the family business when she was seven. After years of working in the family business part-time and having completed her studies at Stirling University, Babson College, Harvard University and the University of Limerick, Naomi established her own consulting business, consulting family businesses in her hometown. She is now a Professor of Entrepreneurship and Business Innovation at Griffith University, teaching future family business leaders and researching family business issues as well. Naomi is an award-winning academic having received numerous awards for her teaching and her research.

Associate Professor Rob Hales is the discipline leader for Sustainable Business and Management in the Department of Business Strategy and Innovation. His research interests focus on the governance issues around the grand challenges of our time. Furthermore, his research focuses on SDGs in business and government, a business case for climate change, climate change policy, carbon management, sustainable tourism and working with First Peoples on consent processes and climate change. He was the first programme director of Griffith University's Master of Global Development. He teaches in the Department of Business Strategy and Innovation and has convened master's level courses such as Leadership for Sustainable Business, Research Methods for Policy Makers and Sustainability and Systems Thinking. He supervises PhD students in the areas of collaborative governance, sustainability transitions and climate change.

About the Contributors

Alejandro (Alec) Delaney is Argentina-born. He has a Doctorate in Business administration, an MBA, and is a veterinarian (DVM). He has over 35 years of experience in International Business and has lived and worked in several countries and cities, including Hong Kong, Mexico, Buenos Aires and Miami. He is also an investor in biotechnological projects, a livestock producer and a Professor of International Negotiation at Florida International University (FIU).

Josephine Igoe is a Lecturer in the areas of International Business Strategy and Entrepreneurship at University of Galway, Ireland. She has won several best-paper awards and publishes and supervises PhD students in these areas.

Filzah Md Isa is currently an Associate Professor at the Taylors University Lakeside Campus Malaysia. She has teaching experience of almost 30 years, both in public and private universities. She has published numerous papers and has been involved in several professional bodies. She participated in many research projects in and with other universities, government ministries and agencies. She was chosen as the 1st runner-up for the Best Entrepreneurship Mentor/Coach for Academia of Malaysia by the Ministry of Higher Education (MOHE) in December 2015. At present she is involved in the Active Ageing and Digital Economy and Business Transformation hubs at the university to produce talents, research projects, papers and networks to establish these hubs as one of the attributes of the university's success in the global market.

Deborah Mireles recently graduated from University of Galway with a PhD in Management funded by the Irish Research Council Postgraduate Scholarship Programme. Her research has won several awards and her dissertation on Multinational Subsidiary Management Behaviour was runner-up for the prestigious Pavlos Dimitratos Dissertation Award.

Shaista Noor did her PhD in Business from Taylor's University Malaysia and was the recipient of Taylor's Excellence Research Award. Her research interest includes women's entrepreneurship, commercialisation, leadership, management, ageing, HEIs and SDGs. She has published numerous papers in renowned journals. She is associated with the World Association of Sustainable Development (WASD) United Kingdom, London as a Country Coordinator (PAKISTAN). She is an International Mentor for the Commonwealth Women's Leadership

Program 2023 of the Association of Commonwealth Universities. She is currently associated with Teesside University, UK.

Rachel Perkins Department of Business Strategy and Innovation, Griffith Business School, Griffith University. Rachel Perkins has a PhD in regional tourism business development in the context of destination management. She is a Lecturer at the Griffith Business School at Griffith University and currently teaches courses that focus on start-up development, sustainable and innovative business management and small business development. Rachel grew up in the small country town of Stanthorpe, in QLD Australia, where she was able to observe the originality that came from small business and became interested in pursuing this focus in her research career. Rachel has received awards at domestic and international conferences and from other institutions for her research.

Markus Pillmayer is a Professor of Destination Management and Destination Development at the Department of Tourism at the Munich University of Applied Sciences. His research focuses on spatial development which he has explored in several contexts including citizen participation, health and sustainability. In the context of his PhD – funded by the German Research Foundation (DFG) – he dealt with internationalisation processes of the tourism industry in the Arab World. He can draw on many years of experience in the international tourism industry and tourism policy, which also benefits him in the context of his scientific activities. In addition, he is a fellow of various scientific associations such as IGU (International Geographic Union) or the DGT (German Association for Tourism Research), the latter he serves on the board.

Nicolai Scherle is a Professor for Intercultural Management and Diversity at the Hochschule für Oekonomie & Management (FOM) in Munich. His research interests are mainly in the areas of economic and tourism geography with an emphasis on sustainability issues, entrepreneurship, intercultural communication and diversity. As a cultural geographer, he has been involved in several national and international research projects, mainly focusing on the internationalisation processes of the tourism industry. He is a fellow of the DGT (German Association for Tourism Research) and the Royal Geographical Society.

Foreword

Prof. Walter Leal Filho (PhD, DSc, DPhil, DTech, DEd)
Chair, Inter-University Sustainable Development Research Programme

The Sustainable Development Goals (SDGs) adopted by the United Nations General Assembly in September 2015 provide a universal call to action to end poverty, protect the planet and ensure that by 2030 all people enjoy peace and prosperity.

They also entail elements of importance towards a strategic business engagement with sustainability issues. These offer a framework which provides businesses with a systematic approach to identify new business opportunities while contributing to the solution of the grand sustainability challenges facing the world today, including climate change. Each SDG, if achieved, will have a direct and significant positive impact on millions of people's lives around the world and the environment in which they live. Businesses have an opportunity to widen the purpose of business through adopting the SDGs as targets for their operations. Thus, they can make a meaningful contribution to the greater good through achieving their operational objectives.

Family businesses are uniquely placed to contribute to SDGs for many reasons. Firstly, because family business models have longer time perspectives, and this allows the family business to link with the longer term SDG time frame – 2030. Second, family businesses often focus on aspects of business operation which do not have an immediate return on investment such as relationship building with stakeholder groups. Thirdly, family businesses tend to rate the importance of ethics higher than standard businesses and thus align well with the social dimensions of the SDGs. Lastly, family businesses have intergenerational perspective which is a core principle of sustainability.

This book provides insights into how family business operationalises SDG#3: Good Health and Well-Being. This book uses a rigorous case study approach for family businesses to detail aspects of their business which help to advance the health and well-being of members of society. The cases provided here are living proof that the family business that operate for the greater good actually work! Non-family businesses can take a leaf out of the family businesses portrayed in this book as they can provide different perspectives on how businesses can successfully align SDGs and business strategy.

Despite many businesses having adopted environmental social governance strategies and environmental management systems, the effect of this activity has not been reflected in a healthier planet. Many 'state of the environment' reports indicate that planetary health is decreasing, and planetary boundaries are being crossed or are about to be crossed. Whilst the cause of this decline is not entirely the fault of business, there still needs to be a greater effort to address the decline. The challenge for family businesses is to use their unique characteristics and set ambitious programs of work that make a meaningful contribution to achieving global goals. This book provides insights into how family businesses can achieve such a mission and how non-family businesses can be inspired to do the same.

Acknowledgements

The Editors would like to thank the contributors of the book for providing insights and sharing learnings from their business practice. We acknowledge that writing up cases in the format required considerable time and effort. The quality of the cases presented is a testament to their efforts.

The Editors would also like to thank Emerald Publishing for supporting the publication of this book and the mission for deeper sustainability through utilising the SDGs.

We would like to thank Mrs Nina Mahnke (Head of HR & Quality Management) for her time, support and valuable insights into the *Platzl Hotels*.

Chapter 1

The Sustainable Development Goal – SDG#3 Good Health and Well-Being

Rob Hales and Naomi Birdthistle

Griffith University, Australia

Introduction

The 2030 Agenda for Sustainable Development, adopted by all member states of the United Nations in 2015, is a shared blueprint for people and the planet, intending to achieve peace and prosperity for all. The Sustainable Development Goals (SDGs) are a call to action to develop innovative solutions to some of the world's most complex, societal and environmental challenges. Businesses play a crucial role in forging this path, and since family businesses account for more than two thirds of businesses worldwide and contribute to 70–90% of the world's gross domestic product (GDP), we believe it is important to showcase the role they play in facilitating the achievement of these SDGs.

The 2030 Agenda for Sustainable Development is a call to action for all countries to address the global challenges of poverty, inequality, climate change, environmental degradation, peace and justice. These challenges are identified by 17 SDGs as depicted in Fig. 1, and within the SDGs are a total of 169 targets. These 17 SDGs acknowledge that ending poverty and other global challenges need strategies that improve health and education, reduce inequality and spur economic growth – all while tackling climate change and working to preserve our oceans and forests (United Nations, 2021).

This book makes an important contribution to research on family businesses by highlighting how businesses can make valuable contributions towards sustainable development. There are several streams of research emerging in the literature on family business and sustainability that are relevant to this book.

Fig. 1.   17 Sustainable Development Goals. *Source:* United Nations (2021).[1]

Ferreira et al. (2021) identify four streams of research in family business and sustainability: family business capital, family business strategy, family business social responsibility and family business succession. The case study approach of this book provides insights into how SDGs can be used to advance the family business's sustainability strategy and social responsibility. How a family's trans-generational sustainability intentions positively influence the strategy of the business and the family's concern for its reputation has been identified as a driver of sustainability in family businesses. Additionally, family businesses routinely combine innovation and tradition to achieve and maintain a sustainable competitive advantage.

During the COVID-19 pandemic, many family businesses have shown to be more resilient and operate more sustainably than standard businesses (such as the shareholder approach). The reason for this lies in family businesses generally taking a long-term perspective on stakeholder relationships and the real need for long-term continuity planning to sustain the people within their businesses. The people in their business are most likely to be family members. However, like all businesses, the COVID-19 pandemic has placed financial pressures on family businesses. One needs to ask the question: *How then can family businesses extend their capacity to operate more sustainably and with more social impact during times of business stress?* Well, family businesses can offer unique insights into how sustainability and social impact can be part of the regenerative response to the impacts of the COVID-19 pandemic. The idea for the book came from two observations. The first observation was that family businesses that had

[1]Note: The content of this publication has not been approved by the United Nations and does not reflect the views of the United Nations or its officials or Member States.

sustainability at their core were performing well despite the impacts of the pandemic. The second observation was that the SDGs were being used as a framework for regeneration after the impact of the COVID-19 pandemic.

The global pandemic of COVID-19 has presented challenges to those working towards achieving the goals. The social and economic impacts of COVID-19 are predicted to increase the divide between people living in rich and poor countries (UNEP, 2020). However, if there can be concerted action using the blueprint of the SDGs, then human development can exceed pre-COVID development trajectories (UNEP, 2021). What is needed is a combination of political commitment from all levels of government, investment in green economy initiatives, socially oriented innovation and a (re)focus on the purpose of business to align with SDGs.

The importance of family businesses in their contribution to SDGs can be envisaged in several ways. Firstly, many family business owners emphasise that the SDGs align with their core values and legacy-building efforts. They use the goals as a chance to align their business activities with a greater purpose and create a positive impact in their communities. Because of the nature of family businesses, they adopt a business purpose that provides a legacy for future generations. This results in a long-term perspective on business development and strategy. Family businesses also recognise that addressing the SDGs can enhance relationships with stakeholders, including customers, employees and local communities. Contributing to the achievement of the SDGs can foster goodwill and strengthen their reputation because of the external focus on global goals as opposed to just their own business goals (Barrett, 2017).

For family business owners who seek to transform their business models, the SDGs are a source of inspiration for innovation. The integration of sustainability into their business strategies can lead to the development of innovative products, services and business models that contribute to the greater good as well as create business value. Family business owners also use SDGs to identify and mitigate risks associated with environmental, social and governance issues. By addressing these challenges as a future-oriented strategy, they aim to ensure the resilience and long-term success of their businesses (Bauweraerts et al., 2022; Muhmad & Muhamad, 2021). Family businesses that are aligned with the SDGs are more likely to have a positive impact on their financial performance (Muhmad & Muhamad, 2021). Consumers and investors increasingly favour companies that demonstrate a commitment to sustainability. Lastly, many family businesses see themselves as ethical leaders and their commitment to ethical decision-making and responsible business conduct is enacted through business alignment and contribution to SDGs.

Book Series Focus – SDG#3

This book focuses on SDG#3, which focuses on good health and well-being. The main targets for SDG#3 are shown in Table 1.

Table 1. Sustainable Development Goal 3. Ensure Healthy Lives and
Promote Well-Being for All at All Ages.

3.1	By 2030, reduce the global maternal mortality ratio to less than 70 per 100,000 live births
3.2	By 2030, end preventable deaths of newborns and children under 5 years of age, with all countries aiming to reduce neonatal mortality to at least as low as 12 per 1,000 live births and under-5 mortality to at least as low as 25 per 1,000 live births
3.3	By 2030, end the epidemics of AIDS, tuberculosis, malaria and neglected tropical diseases and combat hepatitis, water-borne diseases and other communicable diseases
3.4	By 2030, reduce by one-third premature mortality from non-communicable diseases through prevention and treatment and promote mental health and well-being
3.5	Strengthen the prevention and treatment of substance abuse, including narcotic drug abuse and harmful use of alcohol
3.6	By 2020, halve the number of global deaths and injuries from road traffic accidents
3.7	By 2030, ensure universal access to sexual and reproductive healthcare services, including for family planning, information and education and the integration of reproductive health into national strategies and programmes
3.8	Achieve universal health coverage, including financial risk protection, access to quality essential healthcare and access to safe, effective, quality and affordable essential medicines and vaccines for all
3.a	Strengthen the implementation of the World Health Organization Framework Convention on Tobacco Control in all countries, as appropriate
3.b	Support the research and development of vaccines and medicines for the communicable and non-communicable diseases that primarily affect developing countries, provide access to affordable essential medicines and vaccines, in accordance with the Doha Declaration on the TRIPS Agreement and Public Health, which affirms the right of developing countries to use to the full the provisions in the Agreement on Trade-Related Aspects of Intellectual Property Rights regarding flexibilities to protect public health, and, in particular, provide access to medicines for all
3.c	Substantially increase health financing and the recruitment, development, training and retention of the health workforce in

Table 1. *(Continued)*

developing countries, especially in least developed countries and small island developing states

3.d   Strengthen the capacity of all countries, in particular developing countries, for early warning, risk reduction and management of national and global health risks

Source: United Nations (n.d.).

Family Business Contributing to SDG#3

Family businesses can make a significant contribution to SDG#3 through specific actions that align with SDG#3 targets. Family businesses can harness their influence and resources to advance the agenda of SDG#3, contributing not only to their organisational success but also to the broader societal well-being. Some of the ways family business can do this are:

Health and Safety in the Workplace

A pivotal arena of impact lies in the realm of workplace health and safety. Family businesses, driven by their commitment to employee welfare, can proactively cultivate an environment conducive to well-being. Implementing stringent safety measures, offering thorough training programmes and nurturing a culture of health can yield reduced occupational hazards and foster the overall health of the workforce (Bari et al., 2023).

Enhancing Access to Healthcare

Family businesses can serve as catalysts in enhancing access to healthcare by providing comprehensive health insurance coverage and collaborating with healthcare providers to ensure that quality medical services are readily accessible. Such endeavours extend not only to employees but also to their families, thereby improving the foundation of community health.

Promotion of Healthy Lifestyles

Championing healthy lifestyles among employees is another important avenue for family businesses. Leading initiatives that encourage physical activity, better nutrition and mental wellness, these businesses can have a ripple effect of positive behaviours, transcending the workplace and resonating within the broader community (Stier, 1993).

Community Engagement and Local Empowerment

Family businesses possess a unique vantage point to bolster community health initiatives because they are often deeply intertwined with their local communities. By sponsoring health-focused events, supporting local healthcare infrastructure and nurturing collaborations with health organisations, family businesses can have an impact on the health profiles of their local communities (Lumpkin & Bacq, 2022).

Ethical Supply Chain Management and Philanthropy

The pursuit of health and well-being extends beyond the confines of individual enterprises. Family businesses can exercise ethical stewardship by ensuring that their supply chains adhere to sustainable practices, particularly in industries with health implications (Alwadani & Ndubisi, 2022). Concurrently, philanthropic endeavours can channel resources towards advancing healthcare infrastructure, fostering medical research and reducing health disparities (Rivo-López et al., 2021).

Innovation, Education and Awareness

Innovation lies at the heart of health advancement. Family businesses can channel investments into research endeavours, technological innovations and pharmaceutical advancements, leading to improved healthcare delivery. Additionally, family businesses can leverage their networks to provide health education and raise awareness, promoting a health conscious society (Lumpkin & Bacq, 2022).

Long-Term Planning and Legacy

Family businesses are ideally poised to inculcate health and well-being values into their succession planning because they have intergenerational continuity at the heart of their business models. By nurturing a legacy that prioritises employee and community health, these businesses ensure an enduring impact on SDG#3 and its attainment (Gilding et al., 2015).

By embracing the diverse strategies involving health and well-being, family businesses can weave their operations into the fabric of SDG#3's targets. The interplay of sustainable business practices and societal welfare serves to position these businesses ideally as leaders of health advancement. Through a commitment to workplace safety, accessible healthcare, healthy lifestyles, community engagement, ethical stewardship, innovation and education, family businesses can create a legacy of health and well-being that advances the SDGs. The chapters in this book highlight the relationship between family business activities and the broader aims of societal health, thus advancing a healthier and more prosperous world.

Challenges Facing Businesses in the Achievement of SDG#3

Family businesses are well-positioned to contribute to SDG#3 by promoting health and well-being, but they face various challenges in their efforts. Overcoming these challenges will ensure a larger contribution to SDG#3. Many of the following challenges are noted by the family businesses showcased in this book.

The first challenge is about resources. Resource constraints pose a significant challenge for many family businesses due to their relatively modest scale compared to larger corporations. These businesses often contend with limited financial means and a smaller workforce, which can hinder their capacity to invest comprehensively in initiatives centred on employee and community health and well-being. Striking a balance between these aspirations and other pressing demands becomes difficult, given the myriad competing priorities that family businesses must navigate. While pursuing profitability, growth and generational succession, achieving health and well-being objectives necessitates careful planning to harmonise the priorities and multiple objectives (Gilding et al., 2015).

Lack of expertise further compounds the challenge, as the implementation of effective health and wellness programmes often requires specialised knowledge that might be beyond the reach of family businesses. Constraints on resources can hinder the hiring of experts or the development of in-house capabilities to adeptly design and manage such initiatives. Furthermore, resistance to change emerges as a notable hurdle, particularly for family businesses with long-term established operational traditions. Introducing new health-related policies, practices or cultural shifts may meet resistance from both employees and family members, impeding the integration of health and well-being measures.

Family businesses, in contrast to larger corporations, often encounter limited access to networks that could otherwise assist with their sustainability activities. The broader collaborations and partnerships that large companies can establish might not be as readily accessible for family businesses, affecting their ability to achieve health and well-being objectives. Despite their long-term perspective, these businesses also face the pressure to demonstrate short-term results. This leads to the reduced prioritisation of health and well-being initiatives that are not going to bring immediate financial returns.

The distinctive dynamics inherent in family-owned enterprises, particularly concerning family members as employees and potential successors, can influence the implementation of health initiatives. Managing relationships, addressing expectations and mitigating potential conflicts among family members can impact the introduction of effective health measures. Additionally, regulations pose a formidable hurdle, especially in industries with stringent health and safety regulations. Family businesses, often constrained by limited legal and compliance resources, are challenged by adhering to complex regulatory frameworks.

Engaging with external stakeholders for health-related initiatives requires concerted effort, time and proficient communication. Despite their strong community ties, family businesses must devote considerable resources to effectively engage with their communities in endeavours to promote health and well-being. Finally, the measurement of impact emerges as a challenging endeavour, one that family businesses might find particularly difficult due to limitations in tools and expertise.

Despite these challenges, family businesses can overcome them by focusing on their strengths, values and commitment to long-term sustainability. Engaging in partnerships and aligning health initiatives with core business values can help family businesses make meaningful contributions to SDG#3 while addressing the challenges they may encounter.

The Book Chapters

The book series aims to contribute positively to providing evidence of the role of family businesses in effectively contributing to all SDGs. The book is one of 17 vignette book series in which each book is comprised of a set of short, easy-to-read family business cases related to the unique SDG being discussed in the book. The format of the book series allows the works to be accessible to those working in the field beyond academia such as family business practitioners, family business owners, family business advisors, government and business policymakers, members of non-governmental organizations (NGOs), business associations and philanthropic centres as well as to those who have a general interest in entrepreneurship and business.

The chapters in this book focus on businesses that have prioritised SDG#3. Four businesses have been profiled in the book and the first case profiles a company from Germany. The Inselkammer family owns and operates the *Platzl Hotel* located in Munich's city centre 'Am Platzl'. The family members behind the *Platzl Hotels* see themselves as pioneers in sustainability. Many sustainability initiatives have been implemented by the family business. In addition to general sustainability initiatives, employee healthcare plays a central role. The promotion of health and well-being applies to all employees and thus is an important objective of the family business. The family realises that they have many opportunities to improve the health and well-being of their employees and thus can realise business opportunities. Personal proximity to the employees – unlike in large businesses, for example – is considered a major advantage. The introduction of a business health management system in the family business aims to support the well-being of the business's employees.

The second chapter profiles a family business called Noble Care from Malaysia. Noble Care Malaysia has been a family business since 2005 and provides complete care and quality services to aged and ailing community members. They specialise in providing care to the elderly suffering from severe illnesses related to age and terminal diseases like cancer. The leadership of the family business is shared by Dr Ejaz Ahmed Chaudhry and his wife, and their sons and daughters share the position of manager and director. The 'Ageing for All' mission underpinning Noble Care is directly aligned with the SDG Good Health and Well-being (SDG#3). The family business's core values revolve around basic living, medical facilities and love and attention for the elderly in their golden years. An ageing population is a challenge for Malaysia which has limited resources. Noble Care's nursing homes and retirement resorts create employment opportunities for the community, especially the catchment area where it is located. Each centre is estimated to require approximately 12–15 staff. In line with its vision to develop 100 centres by 2030, Noble Care is expected to create more than 1,500 job opportunities. This would positively impact the economy, reducing unemployment, especially in the qualified nursing sector. The main challenge for Noble Care now is to seek novel ways to help the country with increasing demand for more centres.

The third chapter profiles the family business from Mexico called DrugMex. This chapter outlines how the family business evolved into a major pharmaceutical organisation and demonstrates how it makes a significant contribution to SDG#3. The DrugMex company is closely identified with at least two generations of a family, and the family ethos of social justice between the partners has had a strong influence on overall company direction. Additionally, the family and their descendants possess 25% of the decision-making as per share capital. The expansion of the business into Mexico started in 2008 and was officially inaugurated in 2016. Alejandro (Alec) Delaney oversees this plant. There was a realisation by the originally named Dromex,[2] right from the beginning that, unfavourable environmental factors such as lifestyle, geographic factors, poor infrastructure, low health knowledge, lack of education and poverty are some causes of the high incidence of infectious and other communicable diseases in developing countries. From the beginning, Dromex, focused on ensuring healthy lives and promoting well-being for all ages, collaborating in fighting communicable diseases and supporting research, development and universal access to affordable vaccines and medicines. For example, it was the first company in Latin America to produce a vaccine for COVID-19. The challenges for the family business lie not in its capacity to impact SDG#3 as its business mission is directly centred on many of the targets of SDG#3, but rather business succession and geographical spread of the leadership will make decision-making challenging for future business development of the family business.

The last chapter is about the family business called Plant Doctor from Australia. Plant Doctor is a leading family-based company on the Gold Coast that promotes plant, animal and human health through an expanding range of products and services. The family business continues to develop and market eco-friendly products and deliver ethical, economical and effective health and well-being solutions. The case outlines how Plant Doctor provides products and services that contribute to SDG#3 Health and Well-being through delivering economical and effective environmental natural products to promote plant, human and animal health. Even though the business does focus on products for human health offering a range of alternative and organic products, the focus on organic and environmentally friendly plant and animal products demonstrates their mission of healthy places and healthy lifestyles that have a direct impact on the health and well-being of their clients. Challenges for Plant Doctor include the

---

[2]DrugMex was originally named Dromex in Mexico.

cost of organic and environmental products and how the market demand for such products is not as high as cheaper non-organic products.

The Methodological Approach Adopted for the Book

The book used a case study method to gain insights into the practices of businesses using SDGs. The summary outline of the case study template is shown in Table 2. The editors approached a range of potential authors to develop the case

Table 2. Key Aspects of the Case Study Template Used by Authors in This Book.

Vision and mission, services offered by the organisation *Background to the company* *Historical development:* • Founding date • Founder details • Human interest angle of the founder • Quotes from the founder or key people • Size of organisation	*How do the vision, mission and background of the organisation relate to the particular SDG?* • When did the SDG become important to the organisation? • Was there a person who championed the SDG? • Are the SDGs explicitly talked about by staff?
How do key stakeholders relate to the SDG championed by the organisation? • What stakeholders influence the organisation? • Has the adoption of the SDG in the organisation had an impact on stakeholders? • Have stakeholders influenced the actions of the organisation related to the SDG?	*Outline the business model of the organisation and add how the SDG is important.* • Outline key elements • An outline structure of the organisation is needed. • Provide a diagram of the business model • Identify key activities and return on investment • How does the SDG relate to return on investment? • How do businesses monitor impacts?
What are the challenges facing the organisation in implementing the SDGs? *How does the business measure and report on sustainability and SDG activities?*	*How does the organisation see itself concerning providing benefits outside the organisation? What's next for the organisation?*

studies. They approached early career researchers, PhD students, family business academics, family business consultants, managers of family business centres and family business practitioners to consider submitting a case for the book. Interested authors were asked to choose the SDGs·that best matched the family business of their choice and use a case study template provided by the editors of the book series to craft a case study on how the family business advanced the particular SDG. A truly global response was received for the book series with participants from all over the globe.

References

Alwadani, R., & Ndubisi, N. O. (2022). Family business goal, sustainable supply chain management, and platform economy: A theory-based review & propositions for future research. *International Journal of Logistics Research and Applications*, *25*(4–5), 878–901.

Bari, M. W., Ramayah, T., Di Virgilio, F., & Alaverdov, E. (2023). Health and safety issues of employees in family firms. *Frontiers in Public Health*, *11*, 1102736.

Barrett, R. (2017). *The values-driven organization: Cultural health and employee well-being as a pathway to sustainable performance*. Taylor & Francis.

Bauweraerts, J., Arzubiaga, U., & Diaz-Moriana, V. (2022). Going greener, performing better? The case of private family firms. *Research in International Business and Finance*, *63*, 101784.

Ferreira, J. J., Fernandes, C. I., Schiavone, F., & Mahto, R. V. (2021). Sustainability in family business–A bibliometric study and a research agenda. *Technological Forecasting and Social Change*, *173*, 121077.

Gilding, M., Gregory, S., & Cosson, B. (2015). Motives and outcomes in family business succession planning. *Entrepreneurship Theory and Practice*, *39*(2), 299–312.

Lumpkin, G., & Bacq, S. (2022). Family business, community embeddedness, and civic wealth creation. *Journal of Family Business Strategy*, *13*(2), 100469.

Muhmad, S. N., & Muhamad, R. (2021). Sustainable business practices and financial performance during pre-and post-SDG adoption periods: A systematic review. *Journal of Sustainable Finance & Investment*, *11*(4), 291–309.

Rivo-López, E., Villanueva-Villar, M., Michinel-Álvarez, M., & Reyes-Santías, F. (2021). Corporate social responsibility and family business in the time of COVID-19: Changing strategy? *Sustainability*, *13*(4), 2041.

Stier, S. (1993). Wellness in the family business. *Family Business Review*, *6*(2), 149–159.

UNEP. (2020). A UN framework for the immediate socio-economic response to COVID-19. https://unsdg.un.org/sites/default/files/2020-04/UNFramework-for-the-immediate-socio-economic-response-to-COVID-19.pdf. Accessed on July 20, 2023.

UNEP. (2021). Leaving no one behind: Impact of COVID-19 on the Sustainable Development Goals (SDGs). https://www.undp.org/publications/leaving-no-one-behind-impact-covid-19-sustainable-development-goals-sdgs. Accessed on July 20, 2023.

United Nations. (2021). The 17 goals. https://sdgs.un.org/goals. Accessed on July 20, 2023.

United Nations. (n.d.). SDG indicators, global indicator framework for the Sustainable Development Goals and targets of the 2030 Agenda for Sustainable Development. https://unstats.un.org/sdgs/indicators/indicators-list/. Accessed on July 20, 2023.

Chapter 2

The Family Business – Meaning and Contribution to Global Economies

Naomi Birdthistle and Rob Hales

Griffith University, Australia

What Does Being a Family Business Mean?

The study of family businesses is still in its early stages as an academic discipline, and there is a significant challenge within the academic and business communities due to the absence of a standardised and agreed-upon definition of what precisely constitutes a family business. Professor John Davis, a leading expert in this field, has undertaken a comprehensive review of multiple definitions found in the existing literature and has classified them into two primary categories: structural definitions and process definitions (Davis, 2001). The structural definition of a family business focuses on the ownership or management arrangements within the enterprise. For instance, one aspect of the structural definition could be that a family owns 51% or more of the business. This approach highlights the tangible and quantitative aspects of family involvement in the business. On the other hand, the process definition of a family business revolves around the level of engagement and influence that the family has in the operations and decision-making of the business. The process definition looks at the family's impact on the business's policies and its desire to maintain control over the company's direction.

To illustrate the different perspectives, Table 1 has been created, presenting definitions from prominent researchers in the field of family businesses. The definitions in the table have been categorised according to Davis's (2001) classification of structural versus process perspectives, enabling a clearer understanding of the various viewpoints on what constitutes a family business. This categorisation helps shed light on the diverse ways scholars and practitioners approach the definition of family businesses and their underlying characteristics.

Attaining the 2030 Sustainable Development Goal of Good Health and Well-Being, 13–25

doi:10.1108/978-1-80455-209-420231002

Table 1. Definitions of Family Businesses With a Structural or Process Lens Applied.

Family Business Definition	Author	Structural or Process Lens Applied
Members of one family own enough voting equity to control strategy, policy and tactical implementation	Miller and Rice (1967)	Process definition
Ownership control by a single family or individual	Barnes and Hershon (1976)	Structural definition
Two or more family members influence the direction of the business through the exercise of management roles, kinship ties or ownership rights	Davis and Tagiuri (1982)	Process definition
Family influence over business decisions	Dyer (1986)	Process definition
Ownership and operation by members of one or two families	Stern (1986)	Structural definition
Legal control over the business by family members	Lansberg et al. (1988)	Structural definition
Closely identified with at least two generations of a family, the link has had a mutual influence on the company policy and the interests and objectives of the family	Donnelley (1964)	Process definition
Expectation or actuality of succession by a family member	Churchill and Hatten (1987)	Process definition
Single family effectively controls the firm through the ownership of greater than 50% of the voting shares and a significant portion of the firm's senior management team is drawn from the same family	Leach et al. (1990)	A mix of structural and process definitions

This book contains examples of family businesses from around the world, including Germany, Australia, Malaysia and Mexico. There isn't a standardised and official definition of family businesses provided by the Mexican, Australian or Malaysian governments. Family businesses in these countries, as in many other countries, can vary widely in size, structure and scope, making it challenging to have a one-size-fits-all definition. The German Government could adopt the definition as devised by the European Commission as it is a member of the European Union. The European Commission has provided a definition of what a family business is and uses that as the basis to measure the contribution of family businesses to the EU economy. The EU definition aligns more with the process definition identified by Davis (2001). The European Commission (n.d., para.2) proposes that a firm, of any size, is a family business, if:

- most decision-making rights are in the possession of the natural person(s) who established the firm, in the possession of the natural person(s) who has/have acquired the share capital of the firm, or in the possession of their spouses, parents, child or children's direct heirs.
- most decision-making rights are indirect or direct.
- at least one representative of the family or kin is formally involved in the governance of the firm.
- listed companies meet the definition of family enterprise if the person who established or acquired the firm (share capital) or their families or descendants possess 25% of the decision-making rights mandated by their share capital.

Astrachan and Shanker (2003, p. 211) clearly state in their work that because there is no 'concise, measurable, agreed-upon definition of a family business', this leads to a 'challenge in quantifying their collective impact'. Emanating from their research, they created a spectrum on which one could define a family business, from a broad to a narrow definition. This spectrum aims to capture the varying degrees of family involvement in a business and offers different levels of definition, ranging from broad to narrow. Their proposed definitions include the following:

- Broad Definition: At the outer sphere of the bull's eye, the broad definition of a family business is characterised by some level of family involvement in the business, with the strategic direction being controlled by the family. This definition acknowledges that even if only a few family members are involved in the business, it can still be considered a family business.
- Middle Ground Definition: Moving towards the centre of the bull's eye, the middle ground definition focuses on the intention to pass the business on to a family member. Here, the incumbent family members are actively involved in the running and operations of the family business, preparing to hand over the reins to the next generation.
- Narrow Definition: At the nucleus of the bull's eye, the narrow definition of a family business is characterised by extensive family involvement across generations. In this definition, the management and operation of the family business involve representatives from different generations of the family, including siblings in various management roles, and potentially, younger family members (such as cousins) joining the family business at entry-level positions.

These varying definitions within the bull's eye spectrum demonstrate the challenge in precisely defining family businesses due to their diverse nature and the lack of a universally agreed-upon set of criteria. By offering different levels of family involvement, Astrachan and Shanker's spectrum acknowledges the continuum on which family businesses can operate, allowing for a more nuanced understanding of the term and its implications. Van Der Vliet (2021) extends Astrachan and Shanker's (2003) bullseye approach as per Fig. 1, applying it to family businesses in the United States at different points in time, showing the growth in the volume of family businesses over the years.

The lack of a universally agreed-upon definition of what constitutes a family business has led to varying interpretations and criteria used by different writers and researchers in the field. This lack of consensus raises concerns as it can potentially influence the outcomes of studies and research on family businesses. Cano-Rubio et al. (2017) argue that having a single general criterion to conceptualise the term 'family business' would be beneficial in ensuring consistent and comparable results across different studies. The absence of a standardised definition also indicates a gap in the conversations and discussions within the field of family business studies. It suggests that there is a need for more dialogue and collaboration among scholars and practitioners to arrive at a common understanding of the term and its underlying characteristics. Moreover, some writers in the field use the term 'family business' without providing a clear definition, which can lead to ambiguity and misinterpretation of the concept. This lack of clarity may result in inconsistent findings and hinder the development of a comprehensive understanding of family businesses.

Additionally, there can be confusion between family businesses and other types of enterprises, such as small businesses. It is important to distinguish between the two, as family businesses can range from small, local enterprises to large multinational corporations, like LG and Bacardi. Furthermore, family businesses can be privately owned, but there are also many publicly traded companies that have family ownership (i.e. CBS and Viacom). To address these challenges and ensure a more rigorous approach, the authors of the book chose respondents for their research based on the self-identification of the businesses as family businesses. After gathering data, they further categorised them into structural or process definitions, as proposed by Davis (2001), to provide a clearer understanding of the different dimensions of family business involvement. By acknowledging the complexities surrounding the definition of family businesses and taking a systematic approach in their research, the authors aimed to contribute to a more comprehensive and meaningful understanding of this vital and diverse sector of the business world.

Key Characteristics of a Family Business

Family businesses are not homogenous entities, and their characteristics can vary significantly based on various factors. The size, industry, culture and level of family involvement, all contribute to the uniqueness of each family business. As a

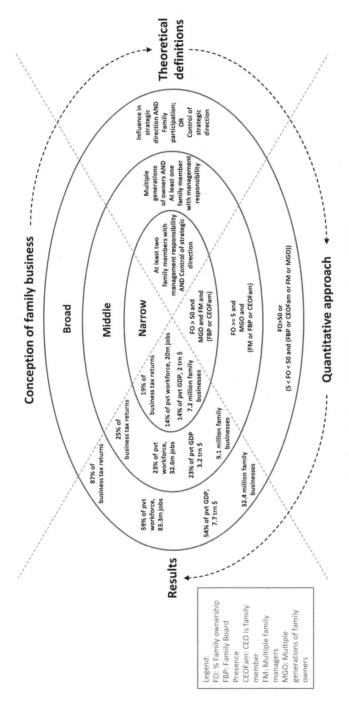

Fig. 1.   Bullseye 2021 (Van Der Vliet, 2021).

result, these businesses may face distinct challenges related to family dynamics, succession planning and finding a balance between personal and professional interests. Despite these differences, family businesses play an integral and diverse role in the global business landscape, making substantial contributions to economies worldwide. Being a family business implies that ownership, control and management primarily rest in the hands of one or multiple family members. These family members have a direct say in decision-making processes and significantly influence the company's strategic direction and operations. The family members in this context are typically those related by blood or marriage.

Several key characteristics distinguish family businesses, including active family involvement in the business, significant family ownership, a long-term orientation with a focus on legacy and continuity and the influence of family values and culture. Succession planning is also crucial to ensure smooth transitions of leadership and ownership between generations. Family businesses often prioritise relationships with employees and customers, fostering loyalty and trust. Moreover, family businesses may have family members assuming multiple roles, taking on responsibilities as both family members and business professionals, creating a unique organisational dynamic. In summary, the diverse nature of family businesses contributes to their resilience and adaptability in navigating challenges and opportunities, making them an important and enduring presence in the business world.

During the COVID-19 pandemic, family businesses demonstrated a notable level of resilience compared to non-family businesses. Research conducted by Bajpai et al. (2021) on a global scale revealed that family businesses laid off fewer staff (8.5%) compared to non-family businesses (10.2%). This ability to retain more employees during challenging times highlights the resilience and adaptability of family businesses in the face of economic disruptions caused by the pandemic.

Due to their capacity to weather crises and make strategic decisions with a long-term perspective, Bajpai et al. (2021) argue that family businesses are positioned to play a significant role in driving the global economic recovery from COVID-19. As the world continues to recover from the impacts of the pandemic, family businesses may emerge as key drivers of economic growth and stability, both at the local and global levels. The findings of this research suggest that family businesses' unique characteristics, such as strong family values, commitment to employees and focus on long-term sustainability, contributed to their ability to navigate the challenges brought about by the pandemic more effectively than other companies. As a result, they are expected to be instrumental in fostering economic recovery and rebuilding in the post-pandemic era.

Family Businesses Around the World

Family businesses are undeniably a reality rather than an enigma. In fact, they are the most common ownership model found across the world and hold significant influence over the global economy. Their prevalence and contributions to the gross domestic product (GDP) are immense and well-documented. The impact of family businesses on the global economy is not to be underestimated. Their longevity, adaptability and dedication to long-term sustainability are factors that have enabled them to thrive and make substantial contributions to economic growth and prosperity. As a result, family businesses are a vital and enduring aspect of the business landscape, and their presence and influence are felt across continents and industries.

As per a report by Tharawat Magazine in 2016, Fig. 2 highlights the substantial contributions that family businesses make to the global GDP. These data underscore their economic significance and the essential role they play in various industries and markets worldwide.

It is evident from the research that family businesses continue to play a significant and growing role in the economies of various nations. Over the course of nearly 10 years, family businesses have further cemented their impact on a nation's GDP, highlighting their enduring importance in the business landscape. In the United States, for example, family businesses contributed to a remarkable 64% of the country's GDP in 2021, representing a seven percent increase over the years. This substantial contribution demonstrates the enduring strength and influence of family businesses in one of the world's largest economies. Similarly, in the Netherlands, family businesses have a substantial presence, accounting for an estimated 276,000 businesses. Their significant representation further illustrates their role as a driving force in the Dutch economy. In Argentina, family businesses have also left a considerable mark on the nation's GDP, contributing almost 1 trillion to the economy. This underscores their importance and ability to contribute significantly to economic growth and prosperity in diverse geographical regions.

Family-owned businesses indeed play a pivotal role in the creation of global wealth and are often significant contributors to revenue generation and economic growth. The joint research conducted by the University of St. Gallen and Ernst and Young reveals the substantial impact of family businesses on the global economy. In 2023, the family businesses studied generated an astounding $US 8.02 trillion in revenue, representing a remarkable 10% increase from their previous findings in 2021.

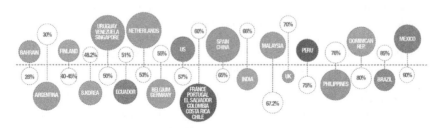

Fig. 2.   Percentage of Family Business Contribution to National Gross Domestic Product (Tharawat Magazine, 2016).

The success of family-owned businesses is further exemplified by some of the world's most well-known and prosperous brands. Walmart, owned by the Waltons, stands as a prime example, with impressive revenues of $572.8 billion recorded in 2022. Additionally, the company employed 2.3 million people worldwide in the same year, demonstrating the scale of its operations and its impact on job creation (Walmart, 2023). Likewise, the Porsche family's ownership of Volkswagen has played a crucial role in the automotive giant's success. In 2021, Volkswagen's total revenues reached US$18.8 billion, contributing significantly to the overall market revenue of US$ 1.8 trillion for the same year (Statista Mobility Market Insights, 2022).

These examples highlight the resilience, adaptability and long-term vision of family-owned businesses, allowing them to thrive and contribute significantly to global economic prosperity. Their ability to build enduring brands and drive substantial revenue reaffirms their position as key players in the global business landscape.

Family businesses have a long history in some countries, deeply ingrained in the fabric of their economies. For instance, the Osaka temple builder Kongo Gumi held the title of the world's oldest family business established way back in 578. Although it ceased operations in 2006, it was replaced by Nishiyama Onsen Keiunkan which has had 52 generations of the same family operating the family business. Some of the oldest family businesses in the world include:

- Nishiyama Onsen Keiunkan (Japan): Established in 705 AD, Nishiyama Onsen Keiunkan is another traditional hot spring inn in Japan (Uniqhotels, n.d.). It holds the Guinness World Record for being the oldest hotel in continuous operation.
- Hoshi Onsen Chojukan (Japan): Founded in 718 AD, Hoshi Onsen Chojukan is a traditional Japanese hot spring inn located in the Ishikawa Prefecture (Houshi, 2017). It is currently being led by the 46th generation of the Hoshi family.
- Château de Goulaine (France): Dating back to the year 1000, Château de Goulaine is a castle and vineyard located in the Loire Valley, France (Chateau de Goulaine, 2023). It has been owned by the Goulaine family for over 1,000 years.
- Barone Ricasoli (Italy): Founded in 1141, Barone Ricasoli is one of the oldest wineries in Italy and is located in Tuscany (Ricasoli, n.d.). It has remained under the ownership of the Ricasoli family for over 850 years.
- Richard de Bas (France): Founded in 1326, Richard de Bas is a paper mill located in Ambert, France (Loison, 2021). It has been operated by the Bas family for over 700 years and is known for producing high-quality handmade paper.
- Antinori (Italy): Established in 1385, Antinori is another renowned winery in Tuscany, Italy. It is one of the oldest family-run businesses in the world, specialising in wine production for over 600 years (Antinori, n.d.).

- Zildjian (Turkey/United States): Dating back to 1623, Zildjian is one of the oldest companies in the world and is renowned for manufacturing cymbals (Zildjian, 2023). The business was established in Turkey and later moved to the United States. It has remained family-owned for nearly 400 years.
- Kikkoman (Japan): Founded in 1630, Kikkoman is a well-known Japanese food company specialising in soy sauce and other condiments (Soyinfo Center, 2023). It has been owned by the Mogi family for over 360 years.

These examples demonstrate the enduring and influential nature of family-owned businesses, contributing substantially to global economic activity and shaping the commercial landscape across various industries and regions. Overall, the research findings highlight the ongoing and increasing impact of family businesses on national economies. Their ability to adapt, innovate and contribute to economic growth makes them a vital and resilient part of the global business landscape. As we look to the future, family businesses are likely to continue playing a crucial role in shaping economies and societies worldwide.

Countries Represented in This Book

The family businesses portrayed in this book come from Australia, Germany, Malaysia and Mexico.

Australia has a robust and extensive landscape for family businesses, with a significant presence in the country's economy. Evidence indicates that family businesses comprise approximately 70% of all businesses in Australia (CoSpedia, 2022). These family-owned enterprises play a crucial role in contributing to the nation's economic strength, generating over AUS$ 4.3 trillion in revenue, with an average annual turnover of AUS$ 12 million per family business (Family Business Australia, n.d.). Family businesses are well-represented among the top 500 private companies in Australia, with a notable presence in the upper echelons of this ranking (IBISWorld, 2022). Within the top 26 companies, 10 are family-owned, with 3 of the top 5 being family businesses.

Australia takes pride in its long-standing family businesses, demonstrating their resilience and ability to endure across generations. For instance, Summerville Farm, founded in 1808, is currently being led by the seventh generation of the family. Similarly, Lionel Samson & Son, established in 1829, continues to be run by family members, and in the late 1800s, it was the largest importer of beers and spirits in Australia. The examples of Coopers Beer, J. Furphy & Sons, P. Blashki & Sons and Peacock Bros. further showcase the diversity and significance of family businesses in Australia. These businesses have thrived over the years, specialising in various industries and upholding a tradition of excellence and commitment to their craft. P. Blashki & Sons, established around 1875 by Phillip Blashki, continues to operate in the 21st century, specialising in producing regalia such as academic gowns, judges' wigs and medals. Peacock Bros., founded in 1888 by brothers Ernest and Charles Peacock, earned a reputation for exceptional quality and service in their small general printing business. These examples highlight the diversity and significance of family businesses in Australia's economic landscape, showcasing their ability to thrive over time and contribute significantly to the country's prosperity.

Germany boasts a rich history of family businesses, some of which date back several centuries, showcasing their enduring legacy and impact on the nation's economy. Recently, it was revealed that the Coatinc Company holds the distinction of being Germany's oldest family business, founded in 1502 as blacksmiths in Siegen (Deutsche Welle, 2023). Following closely is William Prym Holding Ltd, established in 1530, which evolved from producing rolled plates and wires to sewing kits and snap fasteners (Prym, n.d.). Both these companies exemplify the resilience and adaptability of family businesses over time. Germany's business landscape is heavily influenced by family businesses, with 90% of all businesses falling under this category (Schultz, 2019). Renowned brands like Volkswagen, ALDI, Bosch and the Merck Group are among the notable family-owned enterprises in Germany. The Merck Group, founded in 1668, is one of the oldest pharmaceutical companies globally, with descendants of Emanuel Merck's three sons managing the business as general partners.

Family businesses in Germany are vital employers, as they employ 58% of the country's workforce. Although most family businesses in Germany are small, generating less than one million in sales revenue, the number of large family businesses is notably high compared to other industrial nations. Notably, 43% of German companies with sales revenues exceeding €50 million are family-owned (Schultz, 2019). Germany's top 500 family businesses had a significant global presence in 2019, employing over 6.4 million people and generating more than $1.8 trillion in revenues (Family Capital, 2021). This impressive figure accounted for nearly 43% of the country's GDP, underscoring the immense economic contribution of family businesses in Germany. Overall, family businesses have left an indelible mark on Germany's economic landscape, and their ability to evolve and thrive over centuries positions them as essential pillars of the nation's business ecosystem.

According to the study conducted by the University of St Gallen, of the top 500 family businesses in the world, 14 come from Mexico (Bardsley, 2019). Bardsley (2019) further highlights that family businesses in Mexico, which are traded on the stock exchange are predominantly in the Industrial (25.5%) and the Common Consumer Goods (23.6%) sectors, with Services and Non-basic Consumer Goods (18.2%) coming in third. Pittino et al. (2020) quote research conducted by the Family Firm Institute and INEGI – Mexico in 2016, which found that 90% of the businesses in Mexico are family businesses and they employ 90% of the workforce (Family Firm Institute, 2016; INEGI, 2016). This shows how active family businesses are in Mexico and their importance to the economy. A notable family business in Mexico that has got a global reach is that of Tequilla maker – Jose Cuervo (Kristie, 2023). This family business was established in 1795 having received a charter from the King of Spain that allowed the founder, Jose Maria Guadalupe de Cuervo, to sell tequila commercially (Jose Cuervo, 2023). Juan Domingo Beckmann is currently leading the distillery and is the sixth generation at the helm of the family business (Mexicanist, 2022).

Malaysia is a country that is comprised of three ethnic groups across several Islands and includes 13 states (Nations Online, 2023). It has about 33 million people with Kuala Lumpur being its capital city. It is not easy to find data on family businesses in Malaysia (Mosbah et al., 2017), however, according to Cheng & Co. Group (2022), family-owned businesses account for an estimated 80% of businesses in Malaysia and contribute more than 67% to the country's GDP. Family businesses in Malaysia are recognised on a global scale as being key contributors to the nation's economy. In 2017, the Credit Suisse Research Institute's (CSRI) (2017) report put Malaysia seventh globally concerning the number of family-owned businesses. The CSRI report also ranks two Malaysian family firms high. Press Metal: a company that operates in the aluminium industry, ranked 49 globally and 32 in Asia in terms of revenue growth (24% on average) and 44 in Asia in terms of share price return (30% on average). Genting Hong Kong, which is a member of the Malaysian Genting Group, also ranked 29 globally and 20 in Asia in terms of revenue growth (32% on average) (Credit Suisse Research Institute, 2017).

Bibliography

Antinori. (n.d.). *Antinori nel Chianti Classico*. https://www.antinori.it/en/tenuta/estates-antinori/antinori-nel-chianti-classico-estate/

Astrachan, J. H., & Shanker, M. C. (2003, September). Family businesses' contribution to the U.S. economy: A closer look. *Family Business Review, XVI*(3), 211–219.

Bajpai, A., Calabro, A., & McGinness, T. (2021). Mastering a comeback: How family businesses are triumphing over COVID-19. KPMG: United Arab Emirates.

Bardsley, D. (2019). *Down Mexico way: Economics, politics and family business*. CampdenFB. https://www.campdenfb.com/article/down-mexico-way-economics-politics-and-family-business

Barnes, L. B., & Hershon, S. A. (1976). Transferring power in the family business. *Harvard Business Review, 54*(4), 105–114.

Cano-Rubio, M., Fuentes-Lombardo, G., & Vallejo-Martos, M. C. (2017). Influence of the lack of a standard definition of "family business" on researcher into their international strategies. *European Research on Management and Business Economics, 23*, 132–146.

Chateau de Goulaine. (2023). *The history*. https://www.chateaudegoulaine.fr/english-informations/opening-hours-admission-prices/the-history

Cheng & Co. Group. (2022). *Sustaining family businesses through generations*. Wealth Management. https://chengco.com.my/wp/2019/10/01/sustaining-family-businesses-through-generations/

Churchill, N. C., & Hatten, K. 1. (1987). Non-market based transfers of wealth and power: A research framework for family businesses. *American Journal of Small Business, JJ*(3), 51–64.

CoSpedia. (2022). *Why family businesses are the backbone of the Australian economy*. https://www.cos.net.au/c/cospedia/family-business-australian-economy

Credit Suisse Research Institute – CSRI. (2017). *The CS family 1000 report*. https://www.kreditwesen.de/system/files/content/inserts/2017/the-cs-family-1000.pdf

Davis, J. (2001, July). Definitions and typologies of the family business. *Harvard Business School Background Note*, 802-007.

Davis, J., & Tagiuri, R. (1982). The influence of life stages on father-son work relationships in family companies. Unpublished manuscript, Graduate School of Business Administration, University of Southern California.

Deutsche Welle. (2023). German firms with the longest corporate history. https://www.dw.com/en/german-firms-with-the-longest-corporate-history/g-49565958

Donnelley, R. (1964). The family business. *Harvard Business Review, 42*(4), 93–105.

von Dümmler, E. (1881). *Carmen CXI.* MGH Poetae Latini I.

Dyer, W. G., Jr. (1986). *Cultural changes in family business. Anticipating and managing business and family transitions.* Jessey-Bass.

Encyclopedia.com. (2019). *Vaccaro brothers.* https://www.encyclopedia.com/humanities/encyclopedias-almanacs-transcripts-and-maps/vaccaro-brothers

European Commission. (n.d.). *Family business.* https://single-market-economy.ec.europa.eu/smes/supporting-entrepreneurship/family-business_en

Family Business Australia. (n.d.). *Australian family business sector statistics.* https://www.familybusiness.org.au/documents/item/253

Family Capital. (2021). *Top 500 German family businesses – The economy most dependent on family enterprises.* https://www.famcap.com/top-500-german-family-businesses-the-economy-most-dependent-on-family-enterprises/

Family Capital. (2023). *Top 150 Middle East family businesses.* https://www.famcap.com/the-middle-east-150-why-family-businesses-matter-so-much-for-the-region/

Family Firm Institute. (2016). *Global data points.* http://www.ffi.org/page/globaldatapoints

Finnigan, M. (2016, April 22). *Infographic: Argentine family businesses* (66). Campden FB. https://www.campdenfb.com/article/infographic-argentine-family-businesses

Gulf Daily News. (2022, September 8). *Bahraini firms among region's top Arab family businesses.* Gulf Daily News. https://www.zawya.com/en/world/middle-east/bahraini-firms-among-regions-top-arab-family-businesses-l5b2encn

Houshi. (2017). *Welcome.* https://www.ho-shi.co.jp/en/#about

IBISWorld. (2022). *Australia's top 500 private companies in 2022.* https://www.ibisworld.com/blog/top-500-private-companies-2022/61/1133/

INEGI. (2016). *Resultados definitivos.* http://www.inegi.org.mx

Jose Cuervo. (2023). *The number one tequila in the world: Discover our history.* https://global.cuervo.com/about-jose-cuervo/

KPMG. (2021). *European family business barometer.* https://home.kpmg/at/en/home/insights/2022/01/family-businesses.html

Kristie, L. (2023). *The world's oldest family companies.* https://www.familybusinessmagazine.com/worlds-oldest-family-companies

Lansberg, I. S., Perrow, E. L., & Rogolsky, S. (1988). Family business as an emerging field. *Family Business Review, 1*(1), 1–8.

Leach, P., Kenway-Smith, W., Hart, A., Morris, T., Ainsworth, J., Beterlsen, E., Iraqi, S., & Pasari, V. (1990). *Managing the family business in the U.K.: A Stoy Hayward survey in conjunction with the London Business School.* Stoy Hayward.

Loison, F. (2021). *The Richard de Bas paper mill, recognised as a living heritage company.* https://www.printindustry.news/story/36557/the-richard-de-bas-paper-mill-recognized-as-a-living-heritage-company

Mexicanist. (2022). *These are the five oldest companies in Mexico.* https://www.mexicanist.com/l/the-oldest-companies-in-mexico/

Miller, E. J., & Rice, A. K. (1967). *Systems of organizations.* Tavistock.

Mosbah, A., Serief, S. R., & Wahab, K. A. (2017). Performance of family business in Malaysia. *International Journal of Social Sciences Perspectives, 1*(1), 20–26. https://doi.org/10.33094/7.2017.11.20.26

Nations Online. (2023). *Malaysia.* https://www.nationsonline.org/oneworld/malaysia.htm#:~:text=Location%3A%20Southeastern%20Asia%2C%20partly%20on,China%20Sea%2C%20south%20of%20Vietnam

Ozbun, T. (2022). *Walmart: worldwide revenue FY2012–2022.* https://www.statista.com/statistics/555334/total-revenue-of-walmart-worldwide/

Palalić, R., Razzak, M. R., Al Riyami, S., Dana, L. P., & Ramadani, V. (2023). Family businesses in Bahrain. In V. Ramadani, W. J. Aloulou, & M. Zainal (Eds.), *Family businesses in Gulf cooperation council countries: Contributions to management science* (pp. 13–32). Springer.

Pittino, D., Chirico, F., Bau, M., Villasan, M., Naranjo-Priego, E. E., & Barron, E. (2020). Starting a family business as a career option: The role of the family household in Mexico. *Journal of Family Business Strategy, 11*(2), 100338. https://doi.org/10.1016/j.jfbs.2020.100338

Prym. (n.d.). *The company – Prym.* https://www.prym-group.com/en/company/overview/

Ricasoli. (n.d.). *Centuries-old tradition, contemporary excellence. A journey of nearly a thousand years in Chianti Classico Tuscany.* https://www.ricasoli.com/en/

Robertsson, H. (2023). *How the largest family enterprises are outstripping global economic growth.* https://www.ey.com/en_nl/family-enterprise/family-business-index

Schultz, S. (2019). *Dates, numbers and facts: The economic significance of family businesses.* https://www.familienunternehmen.de/en/data-numbers-facts

Soyinfo Center. (2023). *History of Kikkoman.* https://www.soyinfocenter.com/HSS/kikkoman.php

Statista Mobility Market Insights. (2022). *Porche report 2022.* https://www.statista.com/study/60891/porsche-report/

Stern, M. H. (1986). *Inside the family-held business.* Harcourt Brace Jovanovich.

Tharawat Magazine. (2016). Economic impact of family businesses – A compilation of facts. *Tharawat Magazine, 22.*

Uniqhotels. (n.d.). *Nishiyama Onsen Keiunkan.* https://www.uniqhotels.com/nishiyama-onsen-keiunkan#:~:text=The%20Nishiyama%20Onsen%20Keiunkan%20spa,same%20family%20for%2052%20generations

Van Der Vliet, D. (2021). *Measuring the financial impact of family businesses on the US economy* (pp. 1–4). Entrepreneur & Innovation Exchange.

Walmart. (2023). *How many people work at Walmart?* https://corporate.walmart.com/askwalmart/how-many-people-work-at-walmart

Wien, M. (2020). *Familienunternehmen in Österreich 2019.* https://www.kmuforschung.ac.at/

World Bank. (2023). *The World Bank in Honduras.* https://www.worldbank.org/en/country/honduras/overview

Worldometer. (2023). *Bahrain population (live).* https://www.worldometers.info/world-population/bahrain-population/

Zildjian. (2023). *The Avedis Zildjian Company.* https://zildjian.com/pages/about-us

Chapter 3

Germany: *The Platzl Hotels* – Where Munich's Heart Beats for the Health of Its Employees

Markus Pillmayer[a] *and Nicolai Scherle*[b]

[a]Munich University of Applied Sciences, Germany
[b]FOM Hochschule für Oekonomie & Management, Germany

Introduction

Two hotels – the *Platzl Hotel am Platzl* and the *Marias Platzl am Mariahilfplatz* – as well as a diverse range of gastronomic establishments are united under the umbrella brand of the *Platzl Hotels* in Munich (see Fig. 1): In the *Pfistermühle* restaurant, Bavarian craftsmanship and a passionate cuisine with culinary creations come together.[1] The Bavarian inns *Ayinger am Platzl* and *Ayinger in der Au* along with beer gardens stand for modern inn culture with typical Bavarian dishes – always fresh and authentically prepared. Guests experience a Bavarian sense of 'joie de vivre' with spirits from the region, the best coffee and tea in the *Josefa Bar & Coffee*. The *Platzl Karree Boden & Bar* aperitif bar offers excellent, refreshing drinks under the open sky. In addition, seven banquet and conference rooms are available at the *Platzl Hotel*. The *Marias Platzl* offers events of all kinds in the multifunctional event location *Kreszenz – Der Saal*.[2]

Under the management of the Inselkammer family, the *Platzl Hotels* have always remained down to earth and committed to both their guests and their staff.

---

[1]For more details, please check the website (in English) https://www.platzl.de/en
[2]'Kreszenz' was the first name of Inselkammer's grandmother – the conference area is named after her.

Attaining the 2030 Sustainable Development Goal of Good Health and Well-Being, 27–42
doi:10.1108/978-1-80455-209-420231003

Fig. 1.   Exterior View of the *Platzl Hotels*.

All facilities are located next to each other in Munich's city centre 'Am Platzl' – in the immediate vicinity of the world-famous 'Hofbräuhaus'.[3]

Since 2014, Peter F. J. Inselkammer has been the operational manager of the *Platzl Hotels* umbrella brand with over 160 employees, whose family took over the building complex at 'Am Platzl' after the Second World War. The different types of establishments grouped under the umbrella brand are:

- *Platzl Hotel am Platzl,*
- Pfistermühle,
- Ayinger am Platzl,
- Platzl Karree,[4]
- Josefa Bar & Kaffee,

---

[3]'Platzl' is to be understood in this context as the typically Bavarian belittlement of the word 'Platz' (=square), around which the various buildings are grouped.

[4]In urban planning, the term 'Karree' refers to a closed rectangular or trapezoidal arrangement of buildings around a common courtyard. Sometimes, however, the 'Karree' is not completely closed, but has a gap (e.g. passage, etc.).

- *Marias Platzl Hotel am Mariahilfplatz*,
- Kreszenz[2] – Der Saal,[2]
- Ayinger in der Au.

The different types of establishments are managed as a so-called Kommanditgesellschaft (KG).[5]

The *Platzl Hotels* see themselves as pioneers in sustainability. Among other things, short delivery routes take a central role in gastronomy and the hotel industry: long transport routes and the maintenance of cold chains cause immense emissions and are not necessary for the *Platzl Hotels*. The chefs in the *Pfistermühle* restaurant and the *Ayinger* inns are in constant exchange with farmers, hunters, fish suppliers or cattle breeders from the Munich surrounding area. The proximity to suppliers and the high levels of trust garnered from the close relationship with them guarantees the family business the best quality, short delivery routes and thus also the highest freshness. Finished products such as cheese, baked goods, mustard, coffee, tea, jams or spirits come from regional manufacturers and are sometimes even produced exclusively for the *Platzl Hotels*.

Fast fashion or fast furniture pollutes natural resources and leads to massive waste problems. In the *Platzl* businesses, existing materials are restored – as happened, for example, in the *Pfistermühle* restaurant. There, the decades-old ceilings and floors were refurbished, or the upholstery reupholstered. At *Marias Platzl*, flea market treasures such as porcelain plates are an essential part of the design. As a matter of principle, local craftsmen who work with regional woods, textiles and other high-quality materials are engaged.

In the hotel rooms, there are specially designed *Platzl* bottles made of glass, which are reused and thus save around 40 litres of bottled water per day, which is equivalent to around 100 delivered Euro pallets of water per year. But that's not all: to save water, bed linen is only changed for guests with long stays. This has reduced the volume of laundry by a third since the introduction of the measure. In addition, only biodegradable washing-up liquid from 100% recyclable canisters is used in all operational areas.

In addition to employee training and development, employee healthcare plays a central role. After all, the promotion of health and well-being as a universal good applies to all employees. Overcoming illnesses and health problems require the innovative strength of businesses in addition to efforts by society as a whole. Family businesses have many opportunities to improve the health and well-being of their employees and thus can realise business opportunities. The personal proximity to the employees – unlike in large businesses, for example – is considered a major advantage here. The introduction of a business health management system can support the well-being of the business's employees.

---

[5]A 'Kommanditgesellschaft' (KG) in Germany is a partnership in which there is at least one personally liable partner and at least one limited partner who operate a commercial business under a common company name.

Products and/or Services Offered by *Platzl Hotels*

* Personal training;
* yoga;
* wellness massages;
* fitness room;
* discounted conditions in body + soul fitness studios;
* employee canteen;
* staff rooms;
* free cleaning.

Background to *Platzl Hotels*

'*Platzl*' – even though this name first appears in city maps of the 18th century – is a versatile word. The inhabitants of Munich refer to both the square-like street extension and the traditional house located there as '*Platzl*' – those who are nostalgic about it, still speak of the 'Grand Restaurant *Platzl*' today. From the end of the 19th century until the middle of the Second World War, humourous personalities such as Karl Valentin entertained the enthusiastic Munich audience there on the '*Platzl* theatre stages'.[6] Shortly after the end of the Second World War, the entertainment business was resumed, but rather provisionally because the building had suffered severe damage during the war. So, it was no great surprise that the *Platzl* had to close in 1951 due to the danger of collapse.

The Beginning of the Inselkammer Family Era

Given the dilapidated condition of the building complex at the *Platzl* at that time, no businessman wanted to take the risk of an investment. None, except for Franz Inselkammer. The owner of a small brewery in Aying (south-east of the Bavarian capital Munich) decided to rebuild the traditional house. However, the new concept was not limited to a restaurant with a theatre stage. A hotel was to be built at the *Platzl*. The relaunch of the '*Platzl* theatre stages' in 1953 under the new tenants Carl and Hilde Gross was a complete success and paved the way for a successful start for the *Platzl Hotel* in 1956.

Reopening of the Platzl Theatre Stages

When it reopened on 25 May 1953, guests nevertheless found a different *Platzl* than at the beginning of the 20th century. Although the ground plan remained the same, several reconstruction measures were undertaken. For the war-ravaged

---

[6]A German comedian, folk singer, author and film producer. A Munich original, who even has his own museum dedicated to him in the Bavarian capital. He influenced numerous German and international artists with his humour.

citizens of Munich, this was a welcome enrichment or change, especially as it provided opportunities for many comedians to perform.

Birth of the Platzl Hotel

While jokes were being cracked on stage and laughter was being heard in the guest room, construction work continued in parallel. On 9 July 1956, the most modern 200-bed hotel in the city at the time – the *Platzl Hotel* – was opened. Particularly noteworthy in this context was the music from the hotel's central radio system, which could be heard in each of the 200 rooms. This was a technical sensation for the time. Telephone connections in every room were standard equipment.

Farewell to Carl and Hilde Gross

The *Platzl* owes its success during the challenging post-war years not least to the tenant couple Carl and Hilde Gross. In 1973, after 20 years in business and after the *Platzl Hotel* had established itself as one of the best addresses in Munich, the couple left the business. It was continued by Franz and Maria Kreszenz Inselkammer's youngest son, Peter Inselkammer.

Peter Inselkammer Takes Over the Management

Peter Inselkammer came to Munich's old town as a business economist with brewery training and relevant experience as landlord of the *Ayinger Hof*, and in turn, brought about a series of renovations in the *Platzl*. Thus, the hotel was able to present itself with a new look and feel just in time for its 20th birthday in 1976. Changes and innovations were necessary to remain competitive, as the total number of hotel beds in Munich had increased by 35% due to the 1972 Summer Olympics. As a result, Peter Inselkammer decided on a completely new concept for the *Platzl Hotel* in 1978.

The New Platzl Building

An important concern of Peter Inselkammer was that the new building should fit seamlessly into the existing architecture of the old town. Therefore, the historic rooms of the listed *Pfistermühle* were to be extended, the traditional *Platzl stages* were to be preserved and the hotel rooms directly above were to be renovated. Next to it, on the site of the former 'Bockbierkeller' restaurant, the new hotel building was to be constructed. After the design was approved on 6 August 1986, the former *Platzl Hotel* closed in November and the first demolition work began just one day later. In July 1988 – after only 20 months of construction – the first guests could stay in the new 4-star hotel. The official opening took place on 12 September 1988.

The Platzl Hotel Today

In 2014, Peter F. J. Inselkammer, the son of Peter Inselkammer, took over the operational management of the *Platzl Hotels* (see Fig. 2). A new phase of development was initiated – the *Platzl Hotels* have always continuously evolved (cf. Table 1).

Fig. 2.   Peter F. J. Inselkammer, Operational Manager of
Platzl Hotels.

Table 1. *Platzl Hotels* Key Milestones.

18th century	First mention of the '*Platzl*' in various city maps
End of 19th century until the middle of World War II	Restaurant with theatre stage
After the end of World War II	Resumption of restaurant and theatre operations
1951	Closure due to danger of collapse
Between 1951 and 1953	Acquisition of the building complex at the '*Platzl*' by Franz Inselkammer

Table 1. *(Continued)*

1953	Opening of the theatre stage by the tenants Carl and Hilde Gross
1956	Opening of the *Platzl Hotel*
1972	Summer Olympic Games in Munich
1973	Carl and Hilde Gross retire as tenants, Peter Inselkammer takes over management of the hotel
1976	Necessary refurbishment, renovation and conversion measures
1978	Planning for new construction of the *Platzl Hotel*
1986	Permits for new building, demolition
1988	Opening of the new building
2014	Takeover of the management by Peter F. J. Inselkammer
2018	Extension by *Marias Platzl*

The 200 rooms of the *Platzl Hotel* have been continuously renovated in recent years. This includes a Junior Suite and a Bavarian Suite. In addition, the hotel offers six equally newly renovated event rooms, the completely renovated *Pfistermühle* restaurant in listed vaults from the 16th century, the Bavarian Inn *Ayinger am Platzl* as well as the *Josefa Bar & Kaffee* and the *Karree Boden & Bar*. In 2018, the *Platzl Hotel* was expanded to include the hotel *Marias Platzl* in the immediate vicinity of a square called 'Mariahilfplatz' with the associated inn *Ayinger in der Au*.

The *Platzl* business follows the understanding that one must not rest on traditions but constantly develop them further, especially in the context of sustainability. From over 60 years of experience, something has developed in the hotel and restaurant operations that makes the various establishments unique: the '*Platzl* feeling'. An atmosphere characterised by cordiality and respect invites the employees to give their best and helps to shape the family-run business in Munich.

SDG#3 Good Health and Well-Being and *Platzl Hotels*

Most diseases are not congenital but occur during life. People can do a lot to prevent various diseases and strengthen their health. In a society of longer life, targeted health promotion and prevention are crucial at every age. Health promotion and prevention measures address the behaviour of the individual as well as the design of a health-promoting living environment. They contribute to preventing chronic non-communicable diseases from developing in the first place or to reducing their progression, to ensuring that people grow up and age healthily and that their quality of life improves. SDG#3 is dedicated to this issue. This includes healthy living, learning and working conditions as well as regular physical activities, and a balanced diet or recreation (Buzeti et al., 2020; Macassa, 2021; McBride et al., 2019). These aspects and others like being protected from communicable diseases, having access to basic health services or reducing the risk of health crises are addressed by the SDG#3 indicators to ensure healthy lives and promote well-being for all at all ages (United Nations, 2023). Especially in an entrepreneurial context – as also called for in SDG#3.4, for example – it is important to promote the prevention of diseases, mental health and well-being.

People spend a large part of their working lives at the workplace and encounter working conditions that can have a positive or negative effect on their health, depending on their characteristics. Unfavourable working conditions can not only lead to physical complaints among employees, but they also pose risks to mental health.

Healthy and motivated employees are a basic prerequisite for the success and competitiveness of a business. Particularly against the backdrop of demographic change, modern companies have systematically incorporated the promotion of the physical and mental health of their employees into their operational and human resource management and have recognised it as a central issue for the future (Cinar & Bilodeau, 2022; Meurs et al., 2019).

In Germany, employee healthcare measures fall under occupational health management. The aim of occupational health management is to optimise the stresses and strains on employees and to strengthen personal resources. Good working conditions and quality of life at the workplace, on the one hand, sustainably promote health and motivation and, on the other hand, increase a business's productivity, product and service quality and innovative capacity. This creates a win-win situation for employers and employees and improves the business's image as a good employer in terms of corporate social responsibility (CSR). The latter should not be underestimated due to the demographic development and the associated competition for qualified junior staff.

The fields of action of occupational health management include preventive areas such as occupational health and safety, addiction prevention, workplace health promotion, personnel and organisational development. Corrective fields of action are, for example, emergency and crisis management and absence management.

Platzl business has recognised the importance of healthcare and workplace health management and offers their employees a versatile range of services to strengthen the body and mind. The business has recognised, in line with SDG#3.d, that by investing in the health of employees, health risks can be identified and minimised at an early stage.

Platzl Sport With Personal Training

With the cooperation partner *Bi PHiT*, employees have been able to attend 'functional training' once a week in the fitness room of the *Platzl Hotel* since around 2018 (see Fig. 3). The advantage of 'functional training' is that the

Fig. 3. Seal Training With *Bi PHiT*.

muscles are not trained in isolation as in equipment training. This means that entire movements and sequences of movements can be learnt and improved. The training itself is, therefore, much more efficient. The aim is not to build up muscles quickly but to achieve sustainable training, which has a positive effect on the body. *Bi PHiT* is a sports, fitness and health service provider that offers employees individually tailored support through personal training or fitness trainers and therapists. The focus is on work–life balance and nutrition – whether at home, outdoors or at work. Especially at work, sport plays a major role in sedentary work to strengthen the back through fitness exercises and the prevention of back pain. Everyday situations, such as sitting down and standing up, are simulated with a knee bend. This reduces absenteeism due to back pain and improves the employees' quality of life (Shiri & Falah-Hassani, 2017). At different fitness levels, the results are documented, analysed and optimised by the fitness trainer and staff. Weekly tasks and newsletters provide round-the-clock support for the employees. In addition, competent massage therapists from *Bi PHiT* treat deep tensions and take care of the employees' connective tissue, blood circulation and energy flow.

Platzl Sport for Body and Soul

In contrast to conventional fitness studios, the offer of the *body + soul group* (since approximately 2018) includes a holistic course concept: various fitness and yoga courses, cardio and strength training equipment, professional training supervision and personal service. Climbing walls, sports pools and various wellness landscapes with different themed saunas and a professional range of treatments expand the concept. A daily, free childcare service also offers parents the possibility of a relaxed workout. The focus is on a positive attitude to life in harmony with body, soul and social contacts. The employees of *Platzl Hotels* receive discounted employee conditions from the *body + soul group*.

In addition to the offers for body and soul, the following other measures are intended to contribute to the well-being of the employees:

Employee Rates

For employees, their families and relatives, there are special conditions for overnight stays in the *Platzl Hotels*. There is also a 50% discount on the gastronomy. *Platzl* employees also receive various benefits from the cooperation of 'Die Privathoteliers', e.g. reduced rates or exclusive offers via the corporate benefits platform.[7]

Employee Canteen

Canteens increase employee satisfaction. Having lunch together promotes collegial cohesion. Loyalty to the employer increases when employees feel well looked after by the employer (Bhasin, 2018).

Staff Room

Munich is currently the most expensive city in the rental price ranking in Germany. Therefore, employees in the hotel industry face the great challenge of finding an affordable flat. For this reason, *Platzl Hotels* offers its staff accommodation in the middle of Munich's old town, whether for a transitional period or for a slightly longer time.

Free Cleaning

Work and service clothing is not only provided but also cleaned free of charge. This applies to all areas, including, for example, the business outfits of the office teams.

---

[7]On the initiative of various private hoteliers, the cooperation 'Die Privathoteliers' was founded in 2008. Members are privately run 4* and 5* hotels that want to expand their market position through synergies. Furthermore, the cooperation serves for a trustful exchange between the businesses. Through network purchasing and an internet-based ordering platform, considerable savings in purchasing have been achieved in recent years. Human resource management and innovations are further topics that are regularly discussed in the cooperation.

Further Training

Internal and external training courses are offered regularly in which every *Platzl* employee can participate. Individual development opportunities and perspectives are discussed with the employees during the annual appraisal.

The Philosophy of the Platzl Family

'We are *Platzl*' – this is the philosophy that the family business wants to live every day anew together with its employees. A family business where heartiness and tradition take a very important role and where you can and should feel at home. Peter F. J. Inselkammer and his management team know how important it is to be able to develop and have fun both during and after work. With its various benefits and training opportunities, the business supports to the best of its ability, the development of careers as well as personal and professional skills. Healthy, satisfied and well-balanced employees can prosper from within (Winchenbach et al., 2019). The employees want to pass on this positive aura to their guests.

The commitment to employees does not end when they join the business. Existing talents are continuously promoted according to their strengths. The transfer of responsibility, the formation of a personality as well as independent and proactive work have long been part of the (training) concept of *Platzl Hotels* – this attitude should be reflected in the mental health of the employees. In addition, there are events and activities that promote togetherness and fun away from work: '*Platzl* Sport', yoga after work (see Fig. 4), kick-off parties, team

Fig. 4.   Various Health Offers at *Platzl Hotels* Such as Yoga.

events or relaxed summer parties are just a few examples. The physical activities that the employees do together have an effect on the health of the employees on the one hand and, on the other hand, they strengthen the team spirit and the respectful interaction between the employees. Feedback is exchanged at regular team and staff meetings, annual staff surveys or even daily power briefings. This gives both management and *Platzl* employees the opportunity for continuous development. In addition, everyone can post suggestions and ideas on their intranet at any time, express training requests or offer training themselves.

With the outbreak of the global COVID-19 pandemic, so-called appreciation cards were introduced for mutual appreciation to give colleagues a few nice words to make them happy and to contribute to the general well-being. In line with SDG#3.4, this is a manageable measure at first glance, but its impact was all the greater. The employees had the feeling that they had not been forgotten and that they were not alone in their fears. This, in turn, certainly made an important contribution to their resilience.

Business Model and SDG#3 Good Health and Well-Being

The *Platzl Hotels* business model is based on two central pillars: on the one hand, highly efficient revenue management and, on the other hand, a proven commitment to employees.

To ensure that SDG#3 can always be fulfilled, the following values are internalised by all employees:

- The most important concern at the *Platzl Hotel* is to make every guest happy with every visit.
- The high quality of the hotel and the unmistakable *Platzl* character are the great constants.
- To guarantee this, all the people working at the *Platzl* – whether director or housekeeper, porter or receptionist, waitress or bar manager – are guided by certain values and characteristics that are decisive for all of them.
- One of the guidelines for the *Platzl Hotel* and its gastronomy is: REAL.

For *Platzl Hotels*, the attribute REAL is not a platitude but a value that is lived by everyone involved. For the employees, *Platzl Hotels* are REAL because:

- despite modernisation and investment, the tradition and original character of the house have been preserved;
- it is fun to fulfil every guest request – even if tables have to be rearranged, times adjusted or rooms moved;
- every guest is treated equally, and no one has to pretend;
- every employee remains true to himself and is allowed to show his personality; no one is just a number;
- we speak openly and honestly with each other as well as with our guests;
- the employees' word carries weight and promises are only made if they can be kept;
- much is prepared by hand – from the syrups and lemonades at the bar to the 'Spaetzle' (= traditional German food) and sauces in the kitchen;

- it creates trust and the staff feel more comfortable when they tell the truth and act honestly;
- the suppliers are precisely known, and the guests can already read on the menu where the products come from;
- guests can already rely on the freshness and high quality of the food and drinks at breakfast;
- sustainable interpersonal relationships with colleagues, supervisors and guests are to be established and maintained;
- a guest should only leave reception with a smile;
- the employees in the team get along well and also enjoy spending time together outside of working hours to strengthen the team spirit and appreciation for each other.

These values, which must be internalised, can only be lived and implemented authentically if the employees not only have a physical but especially a mental balance or well-being. The *Platzl Hotels* have recognised these central challenges and are addressing them with a variety of measures.

Networks and Awards SDG#3 Good Health and Well-Being

The integration of mental and physical health issues into the existing human resource (HR) management, such as talent management, appraisal interviews or personnel development, has led to several awards for *Platzl Hotels* and the associated recognition in recent years.

Hospitality HR Award 2021

Within the framework of the 'Hospitality HR Award 2021', *Platzl Hotels* was happy to win first place in the category 'HR Strategy Individual Hotels, Gastronomy & Leisure'. This is about new standards at all levels of HR management – from recruiting to training and employee development. The award documents the efforts of a conscious and sustainable investment in junior staff and (long-term) employees, and their physical and mental health. Behind this is the development of a modern employer brand: with courage, inventiveness and good online marketing, the various types of companies have repeatedly made a positive impression. Especially, the employer branding campaign 'What you can do makes us even better. Arrive in the Platzl family!' impressively shows what it means to work in the *Platzl Hotels* and to be individual and authentic (see Fig. 5). Those who can live and enjoy their freedom, feel healthy and well find it easier to work together successfully in a team, according to the philosophy. In a workplace where employees have their roles, receive attention and are respected, people flourish. Only when people are given the opportunity to flourish, they feel comfortable and stay healthy, especially in line with SDG#3.4 and SDG#3.5.

Fig. 5.   Employer Branding Campaign *Platzl Hotels*.

Hospitality HR Award 2018

In 2018, *Platzl Hotels* was awarded first place in the category 'Employee Retention and Development'. This involves a positive working atmosphere and working environment, low staff turnover as well as modern wage policies or flexible working time models.

TOP Ausbildungsbetrieb

These training companies commit to strong guiding principles for high-quality dual training, such as trainees must then confirm the business's statements in an online survey.[8]

---

[8]Dual training is a system of vocational education and training. Training in the dual system takes place at two learning locations, the company and the vocational school, and is characterised by learning processes across learning locations (dual learning). The person in dual training is called a trainee. The prerequisite for vocational training in the dual system in Germany is a vocational training contract. The vocational school to be attended depends on the location or regional affiliation of the company. Most of the practical part of the training is provided in-house in the businesses; the theoretical part is mainly provided by the vocational school. The dual vocational training model is not very widespread outside Germany.

- The business enables an optimal start to the training through an appropriate orientation phase and familiarisation period.
- Every trainee has a contact person in the business who is available to answer questions and solve problems.
- The qualification and presence of the trainers guarantee training at a high professional and human level.
- The working atmosphere is characterised by openness, fairness, tolerance and respect.
- The personality and performance of the trainee are valued, and there is openness to constructive feedback.
- The vocational school is a partner in dual training with which companies exchange and cooperate.
- The trainee is encouraged to participate in work-related projects, competitions and training.
- Trainees are intensively prepared for the final examination.
- Provide timely support to apprentices in planning their careers and further education.
- Ensuring a balance between work and private life.
- Compliance with legal requirements is a matter of course: working hours and apprenticeship pay are based on collectively agreed regulations.

Excellent Training in the Hospitality Industry

Hardly any other industry is as customer intensive as the hospitality industry. This places high demands on employees, which is why *Platzl Hotels* is happy to invest heavily in its junior staff. These efforts have once again been rewarded by the Hotel Directors Association Germany e.V. with the 'Exzellente Ausbildung' award.

Challenges of Working With SDG#3 Good Health and Well-Being

The health and well-being programme is primarily of interest to the management and administrative staff, but less so to the kitchen and service staff. This is also reflected in the regular employee surveys, in which employees are asked about health prevention, among other things.

Nevertheless, the *Platzl Hotels* also try to offer low-threshold offers in the area of health – such as a fascia ball – as a birthday present. For this purpose, there is also a professional introduction to regular training by a trainer.

Business and Greater Good

The *Platzl Hotels* have been involved with the *Nicolaidis Young-Wings Foundation* for years. The foundation's services are aimed at young mourners with or without children up to the age of 49 whose partner has died, regardless of the cause of death or how long ago the loss occurred. These people are in an exceptional mental and emotional situation, which can have a major impact on both their health and well-being. The foundation counsels and accompanies children and adolescents as well as young adults up to the age of 27 after the loss of one or both parents.

What Next for *Platzl Hotels*

Platzl Hotels would like to set further accents in the area of training and personnel development, especially against the background of happy, and thus healthy, employees. An academy for personnel development is planned, which will focus on the topics of appraisal interviews, management, leadership, etc. The findings will lead to individual training that will give the employees perspectives as well as a healthy work–life balance. The findings are to lead to individual training courses that will offer employees perspectives as well as health and mental stability and make a significant contribution to employer branding.

References

Bhasin, H. (2018). Employee satisfaction and morale among the skilled workforce of steel manufacturing plant. *Journal of Organisation and Human Behaviour*, *7*(4), 31–42.

Buzeti, T., Lima, J. M., Yang, L., & Brown, C. (2020). Leaving no one behind: Health equity as a catalyst for the sustainable development goals. *The European Journal of Public Health*, *30*(1), i24–i27. https://doi.org/10.1093/eurpub/ckaa033

Cinar, A. B., & Bilodeau, S. (2022). Sustainable Workplace Mental Well Being for Sustainable SMEs: How? *Sustainability*, *14*, 5290. https://doi.org/10.3390/su14095290

Macassa, G. (2021). Can sustainable health behaviour contribute to ensure healthy lives and wellbeing for all at all ages (SDG 3)? A viewpoint. *Journal of Public Health Research*, *10*(3). https://doi.org/10.4081/jphr.2021.2051

McBride, B., Hawkes, S., & Buse, K. (2019). Soft power and global health: The sustainable development goals (SDGs) era health agendas of the G7, G20 and BRICS. *BMC Public Health*, *19*, 815. https://doi.org/10.1186/s12889-019-7114-5

Meurs, M., Seidelmann, L., & Koutsoumpa, M. (2019). How healthy is a 'healthy economy'? Incompatibility between current pathways towards SDG3 and SDG8. *Global Health*, *15*, 83. https://doi.org/10.1186/s12992-019-0532-4

Shiri, R., & Falah-Hassani, K. (2017). Does leisure time physical activity protect against low back pain? Systematic review and meta-analysis of 36 prospective cohort studies. *British Journal of Sports Medicine*, *51*, 1410–1418.

United Nations. (2023). Ensure healthy lives and promote well-being for all at all ages. https://sdgs.un.org/goals/goal3. Accessed on July 23, 2023.

Winchenbach, A., Hanna, P., & Miller, G. (2019). Rethinking decent work: The value of dignity in tourism employment. *Journal of Sustainable Tourism*, *27*(7), 1026–1043. https://doi.org/10.1080/09669582.2019.1566346

Chapter 4

Malaysia: Healthy and Graceful Ageing for All – Noble Care Malaysia Sendirian Berhad (Sdn Bhd)

Shaista Noor[a] *and Filzah Md Isa*[b]

[a]Teesside University, UK
[b]Taylor's University, Malaysia

Introduction

Ageing is drastically increasing in Malaysia and will continue to grow until 2030 (MHM, 2018; Qandeel & Jehom, 2020). Consequently, senior citizens are expected to be triple and have more mobility, health and care issues that will affect their quality of life (Lai et al., 2019; Phua et al., 2019). The number and demand for ageing care centres across the globe, including Malaysia, are increasing to treat older adults with love, care and attention, similar to home (Noor & Isa, 2020). One family business in Klang Valley, Malaysia, is doing its best to provide holistic care and quality services to old and ailing community members. That family business is Noble Care Malaysia Sdn Bhd. The logo of Noble Care below (Fig. 1) symbolises care for its community.

Background to Noble Care Malaysia

Noble Care Malaysia Sdn Bhd has been a family business since 2005. Noble Care's well-equipped model centres work and provide complete care and quality services to aged and ailing community members. They specialise in providing care to the elderly suffering from severe illnesses such as stroke, coma, tube feeding,

Attaining the 2030 Sustainable Development Goal of Good Health and Well-Being, 43–54
doi:10.1108/978-1-80455-209-420231004

Fig. 1.   Noble Care Logo.

catheters, tracheostomy tube, gastrostomies, colostomy bags, terminal diseases like cancer, etc. Dr Ejaz Ahmed Chaudhary, a geriatric physician, is the founder and CEO of Noble Care (Noor et al., 2021). The business idea originates from addressing his ageing along with other elderly people in Malaysia. Working as a geriatrician, Dr Ejaz was interested in establishing model ageing care centres throughout Malaysia with vision and practical knowledge. He went to the field, realised the problem and pain of older adults in Malaysia and started Noble Care as a human-driven with passion and heart. Noble Care is providing services in Pakistan and Malaysia, and now, negotiation is starting with Arab countries (E. Ahmed, personal communication, NC, May 2023).

His wife, sons and daughters are running the business. It is registered as a mission to support the Malaysian government's social responsibility programme to provide residential care for the homeless, elderly, needy older and unprivileged people. The motto of Noble Care is 'Care and Nursing Services for Elderlies'. Noble Care helps thousands of families suffering from the challenges of caring for old folks in terms of medical, physical and emotional needs. Noble Care dreams of attending to all those old folks unattended at home. Noble Care assists older adults in being mentally vigorous for social interaction, indulging them in different hobbies and interests. It supports them to take responsibility rather than lose themselves in the dark side of ageing. Noble Care provides services to make elderly vulnerable hearts free from inner sadness and silent screams by always surrounding their lives with a balance of support, care, love and well-equipped facilities (E. Ahmed, personal communication, NC, October 2022).

The Clan Behind the Business

The leadership of the family business is shared by Dr Ejaz Ahmed Chaudhry and his wife, whereas sons and daughters share the position of Manager and Director. Mr Bilal Ahmed Chaudhry has been part of Noble Care since its inception, even though he was in college, where he used to help while doing the marketing and other licencing work for centres. Currently, he is the Director of Subang Jaya Centre and oversees the operation of centres in other parts of Malaysia, such as Johor Bahru, Penang, etc. He frequently travels from one centre to another for quality checks and balances and marketing purposes. Recently, Noble Care Malaysia signed a contract with Selangor Government Malaysia to develop five new care centres under Noble Care (The Star Press, 2023). Figs. 2 and 3 show the workforce behind the business.

Fig. 2.   Dr Ejaz Ahmed Chaudhry (CEO Noble Care).

Fig. 3.   The Clan Behind the Business.

Dr Ejaz Ahmed Chaudhry spans a variety of roles in aged care service, such as a board member of the Global Ageing Network (2018) Board of Directors and strengthening the Global Ageing Network's ability (Global Ageing Network, 2018). Noble Care has shown immense growth since its inception in 2005. Today, it employs more than 150 employees and is recognised as the best in elderly care services. Noble Care's motto is providing excellent services in aged care, so the family considers it constantly when setting up new centres. This family greatly supports the Malaysian Government by stressing that nobody dies unattended in their golden age. This simple phrase reflects Noble Care's sincere commitment to care for older people (Noble Care, 2022).

Family Business Philosophy and Family Business Values

The philosophy behind the involvement of the entire Dr Ejaz clan is deeply rooted in the commitment to help the ailing and ageing community for graceful ageing. Noble Care also provides Retirement Resort (NCRR) services at Country Villas, World Racket Centre (WRC), Jalan Cinta Air, Country Heights, Kajang, in Selangor, Malaysia.

> We are pioneers in town for providing the best elderly care services and believe in consumer dignity and informed choices about their care and services.
>
> (E. Ahmed, personal communication, October 24, 2022)

Noble Care offers a self-sufficient, independent lifestyle with more time for the things the elderly will enjoy. Our dedicated team takes care of our residents because ageing is better spent enjoying with friends, family and all the opportunities that our elderlies deserve.
(E. Ahmed, personal communication, October 24, 2022)

Dr Ejaz clan has identified four key themes based on (i) basic living, (ii) medical facilities, (iii) love and (iv) attention that represents their vision, mission and values, as illustrated in Fig. 4. Dr Ejaz Ahmed Chaudhry's Family, who is behind Noble Care Malaysia, is very proud that they are providing the best service in elderly care and helping the Malaysian government to sort out the ageing issues, up to 2030, about 15% of the entire population of Malaysia will be elderly. In line with its mission, Noble Care is keen to develop family-integrated residential care and facilities for old folks who cannot manage themselves at home. Noble Care's vision is to be the best developer and operator of integrated aged care services facilities.

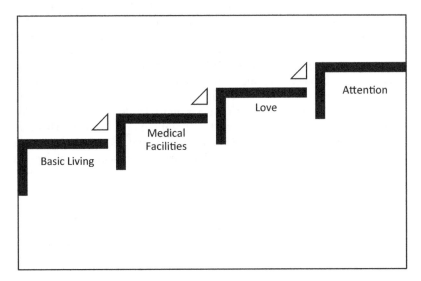

Fig. 4.   Noble Care Values. *Source:* Authors' interpretation.

SDG#3 Noble Care Malaysia

Malaysia requires a maximum of 2000 homes for old folks by the year 2030 as the ageing population will be around 15% of the total population (Phua et al., 2019). Noble Care Malaysia is ready to accept the challenges to assist the government and private sectors in coping with this ageing tsunami challenge in the country. This is evident from the company's vision and mission, which is a blend of development of family-integrated residential care and facilities for old folks who cannot be managed at home. Noble Care provides a blend of luxury and comfort for elderlies in their golden years. The Healthy Ageing for All value of the family behind Noble Care is directly aligned with the Sustainable Development Goal Good Health and Well-being (SDG#3), which is one of the 17 global goals that comprised the 2030 agenda for sustainable development. Thus, ensuring satisfying healthy lives and promoting various engaging activities are vital for the sustainable development of ageing adults in Malaysia. By adopting SDG#3 as its aspiring goal, Noble Care can openly position itself as one of the most reliable ageing centres which offer a complete care service for elderly customers. This is evidenced by the fact that they stress graceful ageing and consider it an essential issue as ageing is a growing global phenomenon. The family business's core values revolve around basic living, medical facilities, and love and attention for elderlies in their golden years. Dr Ejaz's clan focused on the fact that Malaysia requires a better support system for the elderly by ensuring their self-respect of the elderly and giving them a better lifestyle. In line with this, Noor et al. (2022) highlight that Malaysia is one of the Asian countries experiencing an issue of high life expectancy and lower fertility and death rates compared to developed countries where apart from the decline in fertility and mortality ratio, and development and enhancement have gradually evolved over a century. However, in Asian developing countries, the ageing phenomenon grew in a much shorter period. This is an open challenge for a country like Malaysia to cope with an ageing population with limited resources (Phua et al., 2019). Noble Care's nursing homes and retirement resorts create employment opportunities for the community, especially the catchment area where it is located. Each centre is estimated to require approximately 12–15 staff. In line with its vision to develop 100 centres by 2030, Noble Care is expected to create more than 1,500 job opportunities. This would positively impact the economy, reducing unemployment, especially in the qualified nursing sector. Dr Ejaz Ahmed Chaudhry, the founder of Noble Care Malaysia, stated:

> The ageing population has played a remarkable role for the nation in their prime hence it is obligatory for the nation to provide them appropriate assistance, help and care.
>
> (Noble Care, 2023)

Noble Care Business Model and SDG – Good Health and Well-Being (SDG#3)

Noble Care has helped thousands of families deal with the daily challenges of caring for their old folks' medical, physical and emotional needs. Elder care is a responsibility to be shouldered with honour. Apart from providing primary care for loved ones, Noble Care also provides emotional support from trained professional psychologists and consultants to help old folks and their families. Noble Care's niche is to provide residential care and medical support for aged with severe and multiple disabilities who need special care and professional medical services. Noble Care's care services, medical supervision and rehabilitation care for independent living assisted living and total nursing care for the people with severe illnesses, like stroke, coma, tube feeding, catheters, tracheostomy tube, peg feeding, colostomy bags and terminal illnesses such as cancer. Fig. 5 demonstrates Noble Care Business Model.

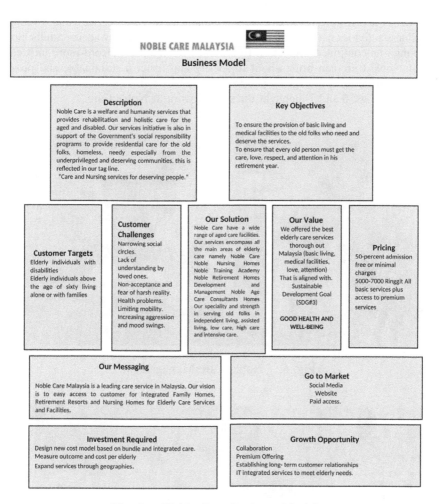

Fig. 5.   Noble Care Business Model.

Documenting Impact – Noble Care Staff in Action

Noble Care's commitment to prioritising elderly customers' health and well-being has yielded significant positive impacts within its business organisation and the surrounding community. Dr Ejaz's passion for elderly care services has helped him to transform Noble Care into a reputable ageing centre in Malaysia. With effective leadership, satisfying care services and a conducive business environment, more successful testimonials of customer satisfaction can be crafted to document its meaningful achievements. Not only customer satisfaction, employee satisfaction and engagement levels have soared, leading to higher commitment that can enhance collaboration with partners and the creativity of its business model. Furthermore, Noble Care's comprehensive care services and routine wellness activities make the centre a retirement place for many ageing adults. So, through its continued dedication to SDG#3, Dr Ejaz can record more impacts that Noble Care can bring about to society and foster a sustainable and prosperous future for more ageing people in Malaysia. Fig. 1 portrays the company logo and Figs. 6 and 7 highlight the staff at work at Noble Care.

Fig. 6.   Noble Care Management.

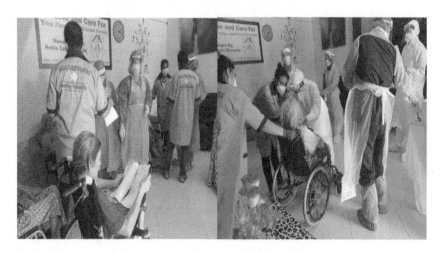

Fig. 7.   Noble Care Staff in Action.

Milestones of Noble Care

Started humbly in 2005 as Noble Care, its mission is to provide family-integrated residential care and facilities, a blend of luxury living and comforts in their golden years, easy access to all the basic living needs and a great life full of love, care, dignity and happiness. Dr Ejaz Ahmed Chaudhry was motivated by his experience as a geriatrician, during which he identified a need for well-designed care facilities. Noble Care started with only one care centre, which provided 12 beds. It grew gradually by developing care centres in the primary states of Malaysia, providing aged care services with the balance of resources and skills supporting it. Currently, 30 ageing care centres of Noble Care are working in various states of Malaysia and offering services, retirement resorts and day care centre services. The facilities include meals, gatherings, recreation activities and some form of health or hospice care. Noble Care is striving hard to change the concept of an Old Folk Home in Asia to a Retirement and Wellness Resort Home and setting into a sprawling area closer to one-hectare land surrounded by lush greenery at the top hill off Kuala Lumpur. Noble Care has revolutionised the concept of retirement homes, creating a lifestyle, resort living with healthcare facilities.

To keep the elderly happy, healthy and dignified in their golden years, Noble Care Retirement Resort (NCRR) gives a holistic view of sitting at the top hill of Kuala Lumpur. The resort boasts a treehouse, gym facilities, Zen gardens and a tranquil rooftop terrace that offers a bird's eye view of the bustling cityscape. They aim to continue to grow, and the quality is always maintained during growth and expansion.

> Old age is not a matter of sorrow. It is a matter of thanks if we have left our work behind us.
>
> (Carlyle, 2018)

Aligning the Family Business With SDG#3 – Good Health and Well-Being
(Ensuring Healthy Lives and Promoting Well-Being for All at All Ages)

SDG#3 aims to seek healthy lives for all along each stage of life; however, the ageing population is drastically increasing globally, including in Malaysia. In 2020, 9% of the global population was above 65 years old, and it is projected to reach 16% in 2050 (Samad & Mansor, 2017). Noble Care stand for providing the best elderly care services, such as care centres, retirement resorts, day care centres and nursing homes. Malaysia's healthcare system yielded excellent outcomes through widespread delivery of basic healthcare services and ensuring 100% attendance of skilled professionals for birth, keeping low rates of maternal, neonatal and under-5 mortality rates and preserving the low rates of HIV and Malaria cases (Novakovic, 2021). Malaysia still needs to work on SDG#3, as the ageing population is an obstacle to attaining sustainability in the labour market, economics, pension and policies. The connection between health and ageing is inevitable because financial stability, social development and protection are mutually interdependent and reinforce components of sustainable development (Phua et al., 2019). Noble Care is striving hard to provide a better support system for older adults by ensuring self-respect for the elderly and a better lifestyle, as in the coming year, existing care centres will not be adequate to meet the expected demand for aged care shortly in Malaysia. More ageing care centres like Noble Care are essential to ensuring healthy ageing among elderly Malaysians. In other words, Noble Care is the most suitable role model for other ageing care centres in terms of service variations, service management and service quality.

One of the proactive actions of Noble Care in promoting age care services is its collaboration with multiple stakeholders and parties in Malaysia to set up more fully equipped ageing centres and daily care services to improve healthy ageing lives among elderlies in urban areas. In addition, more community awareness programmes are essential to spearhead various activities and events involving the public of diverse backgrounds. In line with this motion, Noble Care Sdn Bhd has signed an MOU with the Malaysian Government to set up more nursing homes called 'Pusat Mesra Wargamas' in Selangor, Malaysia. In simple English terms, these nursing homes will be known as the centres of friendly elderly people. This important project implies the government acknowledges and approves Noble Care's establishment in the service care industry.

Challenges of Working With SDG#3 – Good Health and Well-Being

The main challenge for Noble Care now is who else will follow and support their moves in helping the country to cope with increasing demand for more fully equipped and high-comfort centres. Will this be a lonesome struggle for Noble Care or more new ageing service operators can be created from this novel collaboration initiative with the government? Time will reveal all about who will sustain and persevere in the competitive care service industry since it is too early to predict the outcomes of this collaborative effort.

Other challenges that will follow Noble Care throughout its business expansion are related to resources, both human (committed employees) and non-human factors (financial issues). These factors are not uncommon in most business operations. Since Noble Care depends on continuous employee commitment and involvement to serve the elderly customer segment, its human resource department must also be equipped with modern facilities that involve customer relationship management (CRM) activity and software to keep its customer data updated effectively and be less dependent on employees. Regarding financial resources for business growth and the purchase of modern equipment, Noble Care must practice a transparent and accountable corporate governance process that can help to convince more investors, government agencies, financial institutions and banks to fund or provide financial support for its business development.

With unprecedented changes in customer demands and needs due to the advancement of information technology, economic, social and cultural factors, more and better services are going to be requested by elderly customers' families in future. This will lead to another significant challenge that can change the existing management and administrative works at Noble Care. The employees must be equipped with the latest IT knowledge and skills as an added value to deal with demanding customers.

More importantly, Dr Ejaz and his team must also care for their health and well-being to be able to run the business and handle multiple challenges that may interfere with their short, intermediate and long-term goals. Balancing work and health is a tough challenge for someone who is a proactive and innovative entrepreneur like Dr Ejaz. He focuses more on others' needs than his, and his compassionate attitude may deteriorate his health condition at times when he cannot have any control over it.

Nevertheless, Dr Ejaz does believe that older people had done their best in their prime time, so for Noble Care now, they are responsible for doing the best for them in return. With the strong commitment uncompromisingly shown by Noble Care, Malaysians should all realise that elderly people need the utmost love, care and attention for them to age gracefully and healthily in the multiracial harmonious society.

References

Ahmed, E. (2022). Elderly care values: Noble Care Malaysia (Noor, S) [Audio clip].

Carlyle, T. (2018). *Old age is not a matter of sorrow. It is a matter of thanks if we have left our work behind us.* https://www.azquotes.com/quote/48366#:~:text=Quotes%20%E2%80%BA%20Authors%20%E2%80%BA%20T%20%E2%80%BA%20Thomas,is%20not. Accessed on May 20, 2022.

Global Ageing Network. (2018). *Free books library and manuals.* https://ingreso.ittepic.edu.mx. https://ingreso.ittepic.edu.mx/download/94b6e_2018-global-ageing-network

Lai, S. L., Noor, A. I., & Tey, N. P. (2019). *Population Situation Analysis Malaysia 2018.* Population Studies Unit (PSU), Faculty of Economics and Administration, University of Malaya.

Ministry of Health Malaysia. (2018). *Ministry of Health.* https://www.moh.gov.my/. Accessed on January 6, 2020.

Noble Care. (2022). *5-reasons why you should opt an elder care nursing home.* https://www.mynoblecare.com/5-reasons-why-you-should-opt-an-elder-care-nursing-home/. Accessed on May 20, 2022.

Noble Care. (2023). *The best caregiving approaches for the elderly.* https://www.mynoblecare.com/the-best-caregiving-approaches-for-the-elderly/. Accessed on June 30, 2022.

Noor, S., & Isa, F. Md. (2020). Entrepreneurial opportunities for Malaysian women in ageing care industry. *Social and Management Research Journal, 17*(2), 83. http://doi.org/10.24191/smrj.v17i2.10515

Noor, S., Isa, F. M., & Muhammad, N. M. (2021). Managerial obstacles facing the ageing care centres: A case of Malaysian women entrepreneurs. *Vision: The Journal of Business Perspective.* https://doi.org/10.1177/0972262921996495

Noor, S., Isa, F. M., & Yusf, M. (2022). Women caregiverpreneuers A silver bullet for global ageing. In V. Jafari-Sadeghi & L.-P. Dana (Eds.), *International entrepreneurship in emerging markets: Contexts, behaviours, and successful entry* (1st ed.). Routledge. https://doi.org/10.4324/9781003218357

Novakovic, D. (2021). *The World Health Organization Launches the Global Plan for the Decade of Action for Road Safety 2021–2030.* World Health Organization.

Phua, K. H., Goh, L., & Yap, M. T. (2019). *Ageing in Asia: Contemporary trends and policy issues.* https://doi.org/10.1142/10585

Qandeel, A., & Jehom, W. J. (2020). Patterns of living environment among itinerant elderly community in Malaysia. *Global Social Welfare, 7*(4), 383–393. https://doi.org/10.1007/s40609-020-00187-z

Samad, S., & Mansor, N. (2017). Population ageing and social protection in Malaysia. *Malaysian Journal of Economic Studies, 50*(2), 139–156. https://mjes.um.edu.my/article/view/2873

The Star Press. (2023). *Alliances to help sick, elderly folk.* https://www.thestar.com.my/metro/metro-news/2023/05/11/alliances-to-help-sick-elderly-folk. Accessed on May 11, 2023.

Chapter 5

Drugmex, the Family-Owned Company Which Delivered the First COVID-19 Vaccine to Mexico

Josephine Igoe[a], Alejandro (Alec) Delaney[b] and Deborah Mireles[a]

[a]University of Galway, Ireland
[b]Drugmex, Mexico

Introduction

In 2021, amid the COVID-19 pandemic, the Chinese company Bio CanSino chose the family business Dromex to fill and finish their COVID-19 vaccine Convidencia® (Silva Castrejón et al., 2022; Stezano et al., 2022) for the Mexican market. Dromex operates in Argentina, Mexico, Brazil and Spain. The business was named 'Drugmex' for the Mexican operation for name recognition, understanding and language purposes. Thus, Drugmex became the first laboratory to formulate a COVID-19 vaccine in Mexico (Silva et al., 2022; Stezano et al., 2022). Although Drugmex's experience was not in biotechnological products, its technical capabilities and adaptability allowed it to fill and package the vaccine against COVID-19 during the sanitary emergency caused by the pandemic (Silva et al., 2022; Stezano et al., 2022). This case study investigates the origin, trajectory, capabilities and competencies of Drugmex and prospects for future technological development.

Dromex was initially developed in 1990 when Julio Scardigli, an accountant from Argentina, detected an opportunity to act as a commercial agent for two European manufacturers who were looking to sell active product ingredients (API) to local Argentinean generic pharmaceutical finish-dosage laboratories. In 1996, Julio invited three friends into the business to expand into manufacturing and acquire a pharmaceutical factory in Buenos Aires. These friends provided

Attaining the 2030 Sustainable Development Goal of Good Health and Well-Being, 55–69
doi:10.1108/978-1-80455-209-420231005

finance, knowledge of the industry and functional expertise. The three friends were all of similar age (30s) at the time: Oscar Andres, an Argentinean accountant; Oswaldo Ramirez, a Mexican engineer and Alec Delaney, an Argentinean veterinary surgeon. The company is closely identified with at least two generations of the Scardigli family. The family and their descendants possess 25% of the decision-making as per share capital.

The company inaugurated commercial offices in Brazil and Barcelona in 1999. Drugmex' expansion into Mexico was as a greenfield site in 2008, and after some hurdles was officially inaugurated in 2016 as a pharmaceutical plant for sterile products.

This case outlines how the family business grew and evolved into a major pharmaceutical organisation and was chosen to fill and finish the COVID-19 vaccine in Mexico, thereby demonstrating how their ethos and values translate from and to Sustainable Development Goal 3 (SDG#3) (UN General Assembly, 2015).

Vision and Mission

According to Alec Delaney, one of the company partners and who oversees the Mexican (Drugmex) plant, 'The vision of Dromex is to be the first company a pharmaceutical laboratory would think of when needing to overcome a challenge, be it needing an active product ingredient of quality, technical support for registering a medicine, or looking for a responsible contractor to formulate their products. Our mission is to be the best partner in solving the production problems of our customers' (Delaney, 2023).

As a family-owned business, they are open about their ethical values. According to Alec, their mission is, 'based on four main pillars – inspired by their religious beliefs: human dignity, the common good, solidarity, and subsidiarity. Some other auxiliary principles could be added, such as gratuitousness, social justice, the preferential option for people experiencing poverty, stewardship of the environment, social responsibility, and philanthropy'. Furthermore, they believe it is only possible to fulfil one principle by considering the others. For example, the human dignity principle can only be fulfilled by considering, for instance, the principle of justice (see Naughton & Laczniak, 1993; Salamanca, 2015).

Products and Services Offered by Drugmex

Dromex (the original business name encompassing all plants) is a trader and contractor in the pharmaceutical industry. A contract manufacturer formulates finished pharmaceutical products for third parties. This type of service is rare in Mexico. A lack of cooperation between the players in the market and intense competition underpin the business culture for pharmaceuticals in Mexico.

The decision to formulate the COVID-19 vaccine was largely driven by the Mexican government, which tasked Drugmex to manufacture this vaccine, and which Drugmex did willingly. This reflected an alignment between SDG#3b and

SDG#3d in supporting research, development and universal access to affordable vaccines and medicines, as well as strengthening the capacity of all countries, particularly developing countries, for early warning, risk reduction and management of national and global health risks.

Background to Drugmex

The Beginnings and Early Years

The origin of Drugmex stems from Argentina. It is important to note the country and regional context of this business and Argentina's political and economic situation 30 years ago. The hyperinflation of 1989 and 1990 in Argentina under President Alfonsin created the momentum for a structural reformation in the country, which crystallised when a new government headed by Dr Carlos Menem assumed and launched the so-called Convertibility Plan of 1991, which in fact, was a dollarisation of the economy. The changes included extensive public sector reforms, deregulations, privatisation of public companies and removal of restrictions on capital movements and trade (Pou, 2000). Further measures, such as the reduction of import duties and the elimination of restrictions on the importation of goods, opened the Argentine economy, and foreign companies started to show a renewed interest in the region (Pou, 2000).

In this context, a young Argentine accountant, Julio Scardigli, detected an opportunity to launch an operation in Buenos Aires, the capital city of Argentina, as commercial agents of two European manufacturers seeking to sell API to local Argentinean generic pharmaceutical finish dosage laboratories on a free on board Europe basis. Julio rented an office, hired an assistant, bought a fax and named his company Dromex. The agency contracts were vague, as usually happens in those cases (Bradley, 1995). However, Dromex's performance was much above the expectations of the European principal in terms of volumes, conditions and prices.

A factor in the success is that the owner (as in the case of many family businesses) was acting as the salesperson – visiting the customers, closing the sales, and, in the process, setting up friendly relationships with the owners of the laboratories (an essential point in the Latin American culture, see for example, Hofstede, 2001). Eventually, the founder invited three close friends of his – an engineer, a veterinarian and another accountant, all of whom had extensive managerial experience in the pharmaceutical business, to join the business as partners. The original owner kept over 25% of the shares. Given the development taking place in the business, the partners decided to open a subsidiary in Sao Paulo (Brazil) and another in Barcelona (Spain) to cater to the markets of Brazil, the North of Africa and the Middle East, respectively (Silva et al., 2022).

The business operates both technically and culturally as a family business, which aligns externally with the culture of the Latin American marketplace. In terms of the business, Dromex is closely identified with at least two generations of a family, and this family linkage has a mutual influence on the company policy and the interests and objectives of the family (Donnelley, 1988). Additionally, there is an expectation of succession by a family member (Churchill & Hatten, 1987). Also, Julio, who established the business, possesses 25% of the decision-making rights mandated by their share capital.

In relation to the market context, there were some favourable extrinsic factors as well; for instance, the Argentine pharmaceutical market size, estimated at USD 6 billion at the end of the 21st century, represented something like 11% of the market share in Latin America (e.g. Mendoza, 2023; Tanner Pharma, n.d.). Argentina was, and still is today, the third largest player in the pharmaceutical in Latin America after Mexico and Brazil. Moreover, globally, Argentina is the 12th largest pharmaceutical market in value terms (e.g. Mendoza, 2023; Tanner Pharma, n.d.). Another feature favourable to a company like Dromex was that of the 200 pharmaceutical laboratories active in the country, around 84% of them are owned and run by local or domestic Argentine entrepreneurs (e.g. Boni et al., 2023; CILFA, 2021). Local entrepreneurs are keen to use the services of domestic companies, while foreign multinationals usually must follow protocols and limit their purchases to suppliers approved by their headquarters abroad (Bradley, 1995).

A few wholesalers dominate the marketing of the finished formulated product in pharmacies, hospitals and others. Indeed, five distributors monopolise up to 90% of the over 6,000 medicines registered in the country (e.g. Boni et al., 2023). Moreover, those distributors were not independent but sister companies to the large domestic laboratories. Dromex established a solid and sustainable business with those large domestic laboratories. Fig. 1 shows the locations of Dromex plants, including its overseas operations.

Background to the Founder and the Partners in the Business

The founder, Julio Scardigli, born in 1960 in Argentina, is an accountant who started as an API salesman and fell in love with the pharmaceutical industry. Julio is devoted to his family and friends and is a soccer fan. He is interested in travelling and learning about different cultures. Julio is a philanthropist, collaborating

Fig. 1.   Location of Dromex Plants.

with several organisations, soup kitchens and others. In 1998, driven by his vision, he invited a select group of close friends to join what was then known as Dromex. These friends included two accountants, Oscar Andres and Oswaldo Ramirez, as well as Alejandro (Alec) Delaney, a veterinarian. These individuals brought their experience in the pharmaceutical industry, contributing to its expansion both in terms of capital and scope of services. The following table highlights the key landmark events that serve as significant milestones in the development of Dromex and the establishment of the Drugmex plant in Mexico in 2016.

The Inception of Drugmex

The factors outlined in Table 1 played an important part in the establishment of Drugmex in Mexico. In 2016, Drugmex inaugurated its 30,000 sq ft plant in the El Marqués industrial park in Querétaro, Mexico (see Fig. 2 for the Drugmex plant in Querétaro). Drugmex was the only factory in El Marqués, employing between 50 and 250 workers (in the whole of Mexico, there are only 124 plants in this range of employment). The plant possesses the required facilities, equipment and instruments to function under the good manufacturing practices (GMPs) standards required in pharmaceutical activity (Stezano et al., 2022).

Table 1. Historical Development – Some Milestones.

1987–1990s	Dromex was founded in 1990; however, the company owners had started to do some 'spot' businesses together since 1987. Diversification into manufacturing; looking to diversify and reduce risk, the Dromex partners also decided to expand from purely commercial activity into manufacturing.
1990	In the late 1990s, with enormous efforts, the company bought a freeze-dry (lyophilisation) old plant in Buenos Aires, named Instituto Biologico Contemporaneo (IBC), to formulate lyophilised finished products for third parties. Dromex would supply API to their customers and formulate for them through Dromex' subsidiary IBC, acting as a contractor.
1998	The 3 friends/partners joined the business. The IBC plant in Buenos Aires was remodelled and updated, exceeding the norms and existing regulations of the time, knowing that standards may become more stringent. All this represented an investment of USD 5 million in cash and bank loans.
Early 2000s	As IBC became more efficient and ordered, the operation became profitable. Therefore, the partners escalated their commitment to the business by acquiring two further turnkey pharmaceutical injectable plants on the outskirts of Buenos Aires. With those, IBC became a significant player in the Latin American injectable and lyophilisation business and a leading contractor for commercial laboratories.

Table 1. *(Continued)*

2008s	In 2008 Drugmex, with a Pharmaceutical plant of 3,900 m², was started, with production lines of freeze-dried sterile and high-tech injectable solutions, and an estimated capacity of 7 million freeze-dried vials per year and 6 million injectable solutions per year.
2016	Drugmex officially opened its plant in Queretaro, a strategic location in the central part of Mexico, about 135 miles (220 km) northwest of Mexico City.
2023	The company has roughly 300 employees as of July 2023 and is now at a crossroads as regards, selling the business or being taken over by the next generation.

Fig. 2.   Picture of Drugmex Plant in El Marqués Industrial Park in Querétaro.

SDG#3 – Good Health and Well-being 2023 and Drugmex

Drugmex focuses on SDG#3 as an ethos, an underlying company philosophy that transcends all the work that they do. Specifically, Drugmex focuses on SDG#3 Target 3.b, which focuses on supporting the research and development (R&D) of vaccines and medicines, and SDG#3.d, which aims to strengthen the capacity of developing countries in reducing global health risks.

There was a realisation by the originally named Dromex, right from the beginning, that unfavourable environmental factors such as lifestyle, geographic factors, poor infrastructure, low health knowledge, lack of education and poverty are some causes of the high incidence of infectious and other communicable diseases in developing countries, especially among children and older people. From the get-go, Dromex focused on ensuring healthy lives and promoting well-being for all ages, collaborating in fighting communicable diseases and supporting research, development and universal access to affordable vaccines and medicines, which nicely aligns with the goal of SDG#3.b. Dromex is contemporaneous to essential biotechnology developments and has recognised its enormous potential at an early stage.

The belief in helping humanity in terms of better medicines and vaccines is entrenched in all the partners as a culture, who share similar religious and educational backgrounds are very close in age and champion the same values and ideas. The culture of helping people ranges from their overall mission to help with vaccines and health but examples of this ethos can be found in the everyday working lives of their employees – listening to family dilemmas, helping family members gain employment and an overall philosophy of doing good where they can.

The family business communicates both internally and externally their focus on SDG#3.8 (achieve universal health coverage, including financial risk protection, access to quality essential healthcare services and access to safe, effective, quality and affordable essential medicines and vaccines for all), and all the stakeholders receive it well. This communication policy became one of the company's strengths. Employees are very aware of the founders' beliefs, who, even on an operational level, look after their employees' health and well-being in a paternalistic culture.

Latin-American culture has strong traditional family values that transcend professional life (Hofstede, 2001). Critically, according to one of the partners, Alec Delaney (2023): 'A further source of strength of the company is the singular family culture the partners created in the organisation, underpinned by its philosophy in helping people and benefitting the public good in relation to health and universal access to vaccines'.

In particular, when it came to the fulfilment of the COVID-19 vaccine (as will be outlined later in the chapter), under intense pressure and demand for the vaccine, Drugmex stopped filling all other orders and focused entirely on the vaccine delivery.

Latin American Macro Environment and Pharmaceutical Industry Context

In terms of the pharmaceutical industry in Latin America, particularly in Mexico, some industry players argue that Mexico's health system needs to be more articulated and receive more help from the authorities. The laboratories producing generics depend on foreign raw materials for most of their products. There is little development in innovative products and vaccines (CEPAL, 2022). Some scholars maintain that the United States-Mexico-Canada Agreement (USMCA) and the North America Free Trade Agreement (NAFTA) in enforcing patents have limited the Mexican laboratories' vaccine innovation and research and consolidated some advantages for American multinationals (Stezano et al., 2022). Thus, a lack of funding and legal restrictions generated a capacity gap between the Latin American region and other developed and even developing countries regarding vaccine research (CEPAL, 2022).

This absence of an ability to produce vaccines negatively affected the region when the COVID-19 pandemic struck. As of the end of 2021, none of the approved vaccines on the World Health Organisation (WHO) emergency list had been developed in Latin America (CEPAL, 2022). Local governments tried to source vaccines through the COVID-19 Tools Accelerator (ACT-A), and mainly its vaccine column named COVAX, which involved political and financial collaboration between donors, the WHO, Gavi The Vaccine Alliance, the Coalition for Epidemic Preparedness Innovations (CEPI) and the United Nations Children's Fund (UNICEF). As part of COVAX, the global public health community, led by the WHO, established an 'ambitious' objective: to vaccinate at least 70% of the population in low- and middle-income countries (LMICs) against COVID-19, including those in sub-Saharan Africa (Bell et al., 2023; CEPAL, 2022).

Those multilateral arrangements (such as the COVAX and Gavi, The Vaccine Alliance) showed their limitations when Asian producers defaulted on their shipment commitments due to export restrictions in the countries of origin. To deal with the situation, many governments resorted to hasty bilateral trade agreements with the different suppliers of approved vaccines that entailed higher financial costs. In some cases, those deals also raised suspicions in public opinion concerning what they perceived or claimed was a lack of transparency in some of those operations (Silva et al., 2022).

Drugmex and COVID-19 Vaccine 2020

On 8 December 2020, the Chinese manufacturer CanSino Biologics Inc. signed a contract with the Mexican government for 35 million doses of the Ad5-nCov vaccine. The contract specified that the Swiss company LATAM Pharma, an agent for CanSino, would contract a Mexican laboratory of injectables to fill and finish the vaccine in vials (this is to formulate the bulk product into a finished usable product), including obtaining the necessary approvals for the product in the Mexican territory (Silva et al., 2022; Stezano et al., 2022).

CanSino Biologics Inc. is a privately owned Chinese company established in 2009 in Tianjin, China. The company offers veterinary and human vaccines to the market of their development. Their portfolio includes 16 vaccines for the prevention of 13 infectious diseases, including the Ad5-EBOV vaccine for the prevention of Ebola and the Ad5-nCoV vaccine for the prevention of COVID-19 (Silva et al., 2022; Stezano et al., 2022).

Drugmex Became the First Company to Formulate a COVID-19 Vaccine in Latin America

In mid-2020, the Swiss company LATAM Pharma representative, on behalf of CanSino Biologics approached Drugmex. These agents intended to hire Drugmex as a contractor to fill and finish their COVID-19 vaccine. Drugmex, being a contract manufacturing organisation (CMO) with a state of the art factory, seemed a suitable candidate for the formulation of the COVID-19 vaccine because of the condition of CMO and their state of the art factory (Silva et al., 2022; Stezano et al., 2022).

An ad hoc R&D team, integrated by CanSino and Drugmex personnel, was designated for the capacitation and training of the Drugmex workers in vaccine-filling technology. After receiving the bulk active substance from China, the team in Mexico had to stabilise the antigen pH through buffers that included seven other materials (Stezano et al., 2022). Drugmex was subject to several inspections by CanSino's technicians for several weeks. Some investment in machines and devices was required, especially in quality control.

The Cofepris (the Mexican health authority) audited and approved the plant once the required changes were implemented, and the personnel duly trained to formulate the vaccine – Drugmex was the first plant in Latin America to receive authorisation to formulate a COVID-19 vaccine (Stezano et al., 2022). Drugmex had to stop all existing activity within the Mexican plant (and lost many customers in so doing) to concentrate completely on fulfilling the COVID-19 vaccine delivery.

A key issue is the type of capabilities that were demonstrated by Drugmex while filling the Convidencia® vaccine (Stezano et al., 2022), which were as follows: Drugmex was used to work by GMPs and other norms of the industry. Thanks to adjustments and investments, in 2021, Drugmex's production volume was 133% over its original capacity. In February 2021, Drugmex produced 2 million dosages of the COVID-19 vaccine (See Fig. 3). During this period, Drugmex intensified its relationship with universities and research centres. Drugmex showed critical managerial, technical and productive capabilities.

On 12 May 2021, CNN en Español reported that Mexico liberated the first batch of COVID-19 vaccines filled and finished by Drugmex in Querétaro for the emergency use of the vaccine in the country. This first batch consisted of 208,220 vaccine dosages and two retention sample packages with 720 dosages (Lemos & Gutierrez, 2021). On this day, Drugmex became the first company in Latin America to

Fig. 3.   Fulfilment of the COVID-19 Vaccine at Drugmex.

formulate a COVID-19 vaccine. On 22 March 2021, the first vaccines left the Drugmex plant under armed guard (see Figs. 4 and 5). Such was the significance of the vaccine to the Mexican people at the height of the COVID-19 pandemic.

Fig. 4.   The First COVID-19 Vaccines Packaged in Mexico Leave the Drugmex Plant.

Fig. 5.   First Vaccines Leave DrugMex on 22 March 2021.

Drugmex Business Model and SDG#3 Target 3.3, Target 3.b and Target 3.d

The Pharma industry has two 'camps' essentially; the developers e.g. Pfizer, and the generics, the latter of which can sell medicines for 30% of the price of original developers. The view of Drugmex in developing generics is, according to Alec Delaney (partner and head of Drugmex), 'We help with the price of medicines. We do not sell only to certain customers, even if we are asked to do so – we want to be fair and help the public'. Also, he states, 'Dromex and Drugmex supply generic medicines as cheaply as possible in interests of fairness for all people'. This has been a key element and philosophy of their business over the years. Therefore, there is a strong link to SDG#3, in particular target 3.b, and target 3.d providing access to medicines for all for the management of global health risks.

Technically, the business model of Dromex and subsequently Drugmex involves three key activities as described below. However, each of these activities had to cease to fulfil the COVID-19 vaccine completely from 2020. This loss was incurred directly by Drugmex:

(1) Trading of drugs – reselling drugs to customers and suppliers (mostly Chinese and Indian customers). This is the most profitable part of the business, with profitability between 5–30%, averaging around 20% profitability.

(2) The second key activity of the business is consulting, using its industry knowledge, and working with customers for product development as cheaply as possible, for example, using its small R&D lab in Buenos Aires (Innova

lab), which in turn will purchase the API for 5–6 years in payment. This element of the business is really to help and develop medicines for the benefit of the public good, aligning to SDG#3 Target 3.b once again, ensuring affordable medicines to all.

(3) The final activity of the business is the factory, which is the least profitable element. It is a very demanding business due to regulatory requirements. However, it has an important prestige for the business as it manufactures products for the customer.

The values, mission and overall work environment are strongly paternalistic, as is common in Latin American culture. This means that the company is quite involved in the personal family issues of employees. This, in turn, promotes a need to not just provide for, but listen to and treat employees as key stakeholders in the overall values of the business. This approach is reflected in smaller practices, such as employing family members, addressing various family problems that may arise and treating employees as part of the overall business family. These actions align not only with SDG#3 but also have a tangible and meaningful impact on employees' everyday experiences.

In terms of major impacts, the vaccine fulfilled by Drugmex did not have the same freezing requirements as other vaccines and did not require below-temperature freezing methods. This meant that the vaccine could be distributed to very isolated and rural towns and cities in Mexico. Consequently, many everyday people benefitted, particularly in a context where wealthy people wished to pay 10,000 USD for a vaccine at this time in 2020 during the pandemic. The vaccination campaign against COVID-19 in Mexico began at the end of December 2020. Over two years later, around 76% of the country's population had been administered at least one dose of the vaccine. By that same date, more than 64% of Mexican inhabitants had received the recommended amount of doses for immunisation.

Drugmex also partners with local universities in Mexico to develop and train scientists and key employees to help develop and grow the business. However, Drugmex does not measure some of these impacts, as the activities are seen as routine and form part of Drugmex's paternalistic culture, a philosophy underpinned by the management style of the owners.

In terms of understanding the impact and goals of SDG#3, it is important to consider the economic context of Argentina and Latin America. In some respects, private industry competes with the government in terms of its ability to be responsive to social needs and impact on society. Many multinationals, indeed, do not enter Latin America. Dromex (and Drugmex) give to society not only in terms of their product development at as low a cost as possible, and as evidenced by the fulfilment of the COVID-19 vaccine, as needed but it also undertakes extensive charity work in all areas of society underpinned by its social justice beliefs. This shows Drugmex's attempt to achieve SDG#3.8, which seeks to provide affordable essential medicines and vaccines for all. The company has extensive experience and time spent in navigating government and social needs. The ethos and values of the three partners, which transcend the culture of the business, in this paternalistic environment, means that there was no resistance by employees or from within society to pursuing the SDG goal. Indeed, post-COVID-19 vaccine, the Drugmex plant, which had sacrificed all of its 'regular' customer base to provide 100% capacity for fulfilment of the COVID-19 vaccine, was left to pick up its business where it left off after the vaccine fulfilment was complete. This, of course, was a major challenge for the business; however, the value of working for the greater good has meant that the business remains fully capable of sustaining itself into the future.

Next Steps for Drugmex

The role that Drugmex played during the pandemic with the COVID-19 vaccine was a boost to the prestige of the Dromex group. Nevertheless, the situation finds the four core founders of Dromex in their sixties, living in four different countries, all with adult children. Some of the offspring are interested in the pharmaceutical business and working for the group, and some are not. Latin America's economic and political situation has become more volatile than in previous times. On the other hand, the pharmaceutical industry is changing with the emergence of three new business models: (a) companies that may be active in several therapeutic areas but are quickly divesting parts of their portfolio and acquiring new ones; (b) the data-rich virtual pharmaceutical player, offering solutions through healthcare platforms and (c) the niche player focusing on a single disease looking at the entire patient pathway from prevention to cure, stressing the prevention (KPMG, 2019). Many products will become obsolete shortly as monoclonal antibody therapies replace traditional drugs of all types, from oncological to antibiotics.

Dromex and Drugmex used to presume that they could make quick decisions, avoiding the drawbacks of large pharmaceuticals. However, at this point, the company's owners are all in the early mid 60s age group and find themselves at a crossroads that will define their future and, perhaps critically, the future values of the business. Julio's son is keen to continue the business. The next generation has their views on how to run the business, not necessarily underpinned by the same values as the founders. As of July 2023, it looks as if the business may be sold.

References

Bell, D. A., Brown, G. W., Oyibo, W., Ouédraogo, S., Tacheva, B., Barbaud, E., Kalk, A., Ridde, V., & Paul, E. (2023). COVAX – Time to reconsider the strategy and its target. *Health Policy Open, 4*, 100096. https://doi.org/10.1016/j.hpopen.2023.100096

Boni, S., Marin, G. H., Tarragona, S., Limeres, M., & Garay, V. (2023). Caracterización de la oferta de medicamentos en la República Argentina. *Medicina (Buenos Aires), 83*. https://bit.ly/3BpKTYL

Bradley, F. (1995). *International marketing strategy* (2nd ed.). Prentice Hall International (UK) Ltd.

CEPAL, N. (2022). *Report of the Third meeting of the Conference on Science, Innovation and Information and Communications Technologies of the Economic Commission for Latin America and the Caribbean.* Repositorio CEPAL. https://repositorio.cepal.org/bitstream/handle/11362/47968/1/S2200532_en.pdf. Accessed on June 29, 2023.

Churchill, N., & Hatten, K. J. (1987). Non-market-based transfers of wealth and power: A research framework for family businesses. *American Journal of Small Business, 11*(3), 51–64. https://doi.org/10.1177/104225878701100305

CILFA. (2021). *Scenario and perspectives for the national pharmaceutical industry 2021–2025.* CILFA Industrial Chamber of Argentine Pharmaceutical Laboratories. https://cilfa.org.ar/wp1/wp-content/uploads/2021/08/Escenario-y-Perspectivas-de-la-Industria-Farmaceutica-Argentina-Ingles-2021.pdf. Accessed on August 20, 2023.

Donnelley, R. G. (1988). The family business. *Family Business Review, 1*(4), 427–445. https://doi.org/10.1111/j.1741-6248.1988.00427.x

Hofstede, G. (2001). *Culture's consequences: Comparing values, behaviors, institutions and organisations across nations.* Sage.

KPMG. (2019). *Reshaping the future of pharma.* KPMG. https://assets.kpmg.com/content/dam/kpmg/uk/pdf/2019/04/reshaping-the-future-of-pharma.pdf. Accessed on August 10, 2023.

Lemos, G., & Gutierrez, F. (2021). *México libera lote de vacuna de Cansino contra el COVID-19.* CNN Español. https://cnnespanol.cnn.com/2021/05/12/mexico-libera-lote-vacuna-cansino-COVID-19-orix/. Accessed on May 12, 2023.

Mendoza, J. (2023). *Pharmaceutical industry in Argentina – Statistics & Facts.* Statista. https://www.statista.com/topics/10650/pharmaceutical-industry-in-argentina/#topicOverview. Accessed on June 16, 2023.

Naughton, M., & Laczniak, G. R. (1993). A theological context of work from the Catholic Social Encyclical Tradition. *Journal of Business Ethics, 12*(12), 981–994. https://doi.org/10.1007/bf00871718

Pou, P. (2000). Argentina's Structural Reforms of the 1990s. *Finance & Development, 37*(1), 13. https://www.imf.org/external/pubs/ft/fandd/2000/03/pou.htm. Accessed on March 20, 2023.

Salamanca, A. M. (2015). Managing people humanly: Some Catholic social teaching considerations for human resource management. In *The International conference on Catholic social thought and management education.* Ateneo de Manila University. https://sites.gmercyu.edu/catholic-social/wp-content/uploads/sites/45/2018/01/human-resource-mgmt.pdf

Silva, D., Castrejón, D., Lamberti, M. J., & Camacho, S. (2022). *El negocio de las vacunas.* CDMX: PODER. https://poderlatam.org/wp-content/uploads/2022/06/Negocio_De_Vacunas_Reporte_Escrito.pdf. Accessed on June 20, 2023.

Stezano, F., Oliver Espinoza, R., & Gómez, J. (2022). Capacidades del sector biofarmacéutico mexicano. Proceso de envasado de la vacuna Convidencia® por la empresa Drugmex. In M. Versino & P. Elinbaum (Eds.), *Nuevas configuraciones territoriales y paradigmas tecno-económicos en América Latina.* Ediciones Z. http://jornadasceur.conicet.gov.ar/archivos/Versino_Elinbaum_2022_Libro_JC23.pdf

Tanner Pharma. (n.d.). *A Guide to the Key Pharma Markets in Latin America*. Tanner Pharma. https://tannerpharma.com/wp-content/uploads/2022/10/LAC-A-Guide-to-the-Key-Pharma-Markets-in-LATAM.pd. Accessed on August 10, 2023.

UN General Assembly. (2015). *Transforming our world: The 2030 Agenda for Sustainable Development*. United Nations. https://documents-dds-ny.un.org/doc/UNDOC/GEN/N15/291/89/PDF/N1529189.pdf?OpenElement. Accessed on September 25, 2022.

Chapter 6

Australia: Advancing Health and Sustainability: The Case of Plant Doctor

Rachel Perkins

Griffith University, Australia

Introduction

Plant Doctor is a leading family-based company on the Gold Coast that promotes plant, animal and human health through an expanding range of products and services. The family business continues to develop and market eco-friendly products and deliver ethical, economical and effective health and well-being solutions. Plant Doctor's clientele includes garden and lawn enthusiasts, organic and sustainability-focused people and pet owners and health-conscious individuals seeking alternative health supplements. The owner of the family business is Adam Fitzhenry. Plant Doctor is the legacy of the late Daniel Fitzhenry whose vision was to combine the best of both traditional and organic ingredients to formulate premium products that were ahead of their time. His vision saw him combining the best of both traditional and organic ingredients to formulate premium products that were ahead of their time and have since become the benchmark. The case aims to outline how the Plant Doctor provides products and services that contribute to Sustainable Development Goal 3 (SDG#3) Health and Well-being through delivering economical and effective environmental natural products to promote plant, human and animal health. Fig. 1 shows the owner and staff of Plant Doctor.

The Mission of Plant Doctor

Plant Doctor's original focus was manufacturing and supplying an exceptional range of environmentally friendly fertilisers and soil conditioners designed to suit Australian conditions. However, the family-based company has shifted its focus

Attaining the 2030 Sustainable Development Goal of Good Health and Well-Being, 71–82
doi:10.1108/978-1-80455-209-420231006

Fig. 1.   The Owner Adam Fitzhenry (Centred) and the Staff of Plant Doctor.

towards plant, animal and human health. The mission of Plant Doctor is to develop and market eco-friendly products that deliver ethical, economical and effective health and well-being solutions.

Products and Services Offered by Plant Doctor

Plant Doctor's loyal customers include garden and lawn enthusiasts, organic and sustainability-focused people and pet owners and health-conscious individuals seeking alternative health supplements. Plant Doctor has developed a range of products for:

- Agriculture, horticulture and hydroponics;
- Turf and landscaping;
- Home garden;
- Animal health;
- Human health;
- Indoor gardening.

(Plant Doctor, 2023)

Specialising in plant, animal and human health, Plant Doctor delivers economical and effective environmental solutions and has created many natural products to help rectify problems with poor soils and promote plant, human and animal health.

Background to Plant Doctor

Plant Doctor is the legacy of the late Daniel Fitzhenry who had worked in the agricultural and horticultural industries for over 30 years. His vision saw him combining the best of both traditional and organic ingredients to formulate premium products that were ahead of their time and have since become the benchmark. Daniel gained his knowledge from some of Australia's largest companies, learning how to source the best products from locally, nationally and overseas. Daniel's eldest son Adam took over the company in 2015 and has continued his father's legacy. Adam's fresh set of eyes and ideas saw the company introduce new retail products to complement the commercial and farming products Daniel had focused on.

In 2017, Adam took over as Managing Director of his father's small company, Agtech Natural Resources. At the same time, Adam decided to further develop the Plant Doctor online store www.plantdoctor.com.au. The company previously had online sales starting in 2009, but under the new leadership of Adam, there was a greater focus on the online side of the business.

The initial focus was to transfer the offering of earth-friendly agricultural fertiliser products into the retail and commercial markets. The business also developed niche organic food products that had small market demand. The business' success in recent years has enabled Adam to bring onboard family members including his sister, eldest daughter, son and two of their partners, to continue his father's legacy.

In 2022, the company decided to split the food manufacturing business from their fertiliser manufacturing to allow the expansion of the group businesses. The companies that are the Agtech Global Group of Companies include:

- Agtech Natural Resources – Imports, fertiliser production/manufacturing/ packaging with a focus on prioritising naturally resourced or organic and organic-based (hybridised) products.

- Agtech Food Manufacturing – encapsulation and packaging of nourishing food-based products to improve health outcomes for users.
- Agtech Freeze Drying – freeze dries, mills and packages, lesser used food stream products (animal offal and undesired fruit and vegetable) providing a value-added product to resell into the market, reducing waste.
- Plant Doctor retails a collection of products our other companies produce or package under their brands or resells some of their client's products as a showcase of works.

The fertiliser company is now known as Agtech Food Manufacturing Pty Ltd. Also in October 2022, the company opened a Freeze Drying business (Agtech Freeze Drying Pty Ltd) to process and supply clients with various long-shelf-life food products. The food is mostly in powder form for their capsule production which is part of the food manufacturing business.

All businesses are family-owned and operated. The companies including the Plant Doctor pride themselves on old-fashioned customer service and aim to make this their unique value proposition. In 2019, 2020 and 2022, Plant Doctor won the Gold Coast Excellence Award for Family Business (see Fig. 2).

Fig. 2.   Gold Coast Business Awards for Excellence – Family Business
for Plant Doctor in 2019.

Since 2017, the business has increased turnover by a factor of 10 and now employs approximately 20 people. The business has 4 warehouses with 3 on the Gold Coast, Queensland and another fertiliser manufacturing warehouse in Alstonville, Northern New South Wales (NSW).

SDG#3 and the Plant Doctor

Plant Doctor can contribute to specific targets under SDG#3, which focuses on ensuring good health and well-being. The focus on well-being is directly visible when entering the website of Plant Doctor. Fig. 3 is a screenshot of the website of Plant Doctor and demonstrates the commitment to health and well-being through their products. It is also a signifier of the unique value proposition of the family company.

Fig. 3.   Screenshot of the Main Page Banner of Plant Doctor Website.

Plant Doctor can contribute to SDG#3 targets in several ways:

Target 3.4 of SDG3# aims to reduce by one-third premature mortality from non-communicable diseases through prevention and treatment and promote mental health and well-being. The Plant Doctor raises awareness about the importance of healthy plants in preventing diseases and promoting the overall well-being of customers. Thus, they have an impact on health and well-being through the types of products they provide and the secondary benefits of healthy living environments. The activity of gardening itself also contributes to mental health and physical health outcomes.

Target 3.4 of SDG#3 focuses on promoting mental health and well-being. Plant Doctor has an indirect positive effect on mental well-being by encouraging people to engage in nature engagement and community gardening, all of which contribute to reduced stress and improved mental health. The food products also have a health focus in terms of organic ingredients that contribute to overall well-being.

Target 3.8: Achieve universal health coverage, including financial risk protection, access to quality essential healthcare services and access to safe, effective, quality and affordable essential medicines and vaccines for all:

The Plant Doctor can promote access to safe and nutritious food, indirectly contributing to improved health outcomes and reducing the burden on healthcare systems.

Target 3.9 of SDG#3 aims to substantially reduce the number of deaths and illnesses from hazardous chemicals and air, water and soil pollution and contamination by 2030. Plant Doctor through the choice of their products encourages organic and sustainable gardening practices that minimise the use of hazardous chemicals, contributing to cleaner air, water and soil.

Target 3.9 aims to substantially reduce the number of deaths and illnesses from hazardous chemicals and air, water and soil pollution and contamination. Plant Doctor has undertaken education and outreach through their news feeds and blog promoting environmentally friendly and organic products. These activities educate communities about the harmful effects of chemical pesticides and encourage the adoption of organic and sustainable gardening practices.

By providing plant health advice, promoting sustainable gardening practices and engaging with communities, the Plant Doctor can have a positive impact on various SDG#3 targets, contributing to better health and well-being for individuals and communities on the Gold Coast. While Plant Doctors does not explicitly state the alignment of their business with SDG#3 health and well-being, they have the mission of SDG#3 at the heart of their business model. The business communicates its mission of the health and well-being of plants, animals and people through documentation of its news articles on its website and posting regular blogs outlining its mission. They also have an extensive social media presence where they not only market their products but also communicate their mission of health and well-being which underpin their business.

Key Activities of Plant Doctor and SDG#3 Health and Well-Being

The key activities of Plant Doctor include sales of products in the following areas:

- Plants and lawns;
- Health and food;
- Commercials;
- Animals;
- Manufacturing.

Plants and Lawns

Plant Doctor offers a variety of natural, organic and traditional products that help create healthier soils and plants. Their fertilisers are offered in liquid, soluble, controlled release and granular formats and include seaweed extracts, and fulvic and humic acids. Plant Doctor offers a variety of natural, organic and traditional agriculture, horticulture and hydroponic products that help create healthier soils, plants and food. Their fertiliser range includes organic, liquid/soluble, controlled release, granular and mineral fertiliser. Importantly for the Plant Doctor's contribution to SDG#3, they offer a range of products that provide plants with insect control and protection through natural herbicide technologies and fertilisers and soil conditioners made from natural resources. This has a significant impact on the health of the people who use these products.

Health and Food

Plant Doctor also provides health and food products. Their Agtech Food Manufacturing products offer customers a variety of natural health products that can be used to improve day-to-day health. Their in-house brand, Nourished Nutrients, includes fossil shell flour (diatomaceous earth) which aims to improve gut health and better skin, hair and nails. It also has micronised zeolite to help remove heavy metals and toxins from the body and humic fulvic concentrate (HFC) to boost the immune system and for general overall well-being. They also stock well-known superfoods such as lemon myrtle, turmeric, moringa, MSM, magnesium oil and neem oil.

Commercial Fertiliser

Plant Doctor offers a wide range of bulk commercial fertilisers and farm supply needs. Their products significantly support plant growth and improve soil and turf conditions, providing sustained nutrition and revitalisation. Importantly for this case, the materials used are naturally based and thus have health and well-being secondary impacts on the people who use the products and the horticultural location where the products are applied. Plant Doctor prides itself on its world-leading technology to produce farm agriculture liquid fertiliser and animal feed and supplements.

Animal Health

Plant Doctor also offers a variety of natural health supplements for a range of animal needs. Plant Doctors state that 'just like humans, animals have varying dietary deficiencies, and we've seen the evidence and the many benefits from our customer's pets and livestock over the years by them adding specially sourced premium organic components into their feeds' (Plant Doctor, 2023). While not directly contributing to SDG#3, the focus on health and well-being in the environments in which people live including their animals (pets and livestock) is important in the mission of the family business.

> Plant Doctor supplies exceptional earth-friendly products to help
> you grow – whether your plants, your animals, or even yourself.
> Our products give you direct access to the science and technology
> driving the agriculture and horticultural revolution that's
> delivering ethical, economical and effective health and well-being
> solutions. Plant Doctor has developed a range of products using
> Mother Earth's natural resources such as botanical extracts,
> humates and silicates.
>
> (Plant Doctor, 2023)

The Plant Doctor positions SDG#3 as a central part of their business model.
Thus, their return on investment is derived from the positioning of health and
well-being in all products they supply, whether that is related to human health or
plant health.

SDG#3 and the Plant Doctor Stakeholders

The Plant Doctor and associated group of companies do not have many stakeholders because they are small to medium enterprises and very much
client-focused. The main stakeholders are customers, staff, key companies in the
supply chain and industry advisory groups. The owner of the family business,
Adam, says that the main influence directing the business model of the company is
customer demand. The demand for organic or environmentally friendly products
is growing and the products and services offered by the company reflect changes
in the demand for individual products, but all are contained within the overall
trend towards healthier products for plants, animals and people. Although
organic products are still more expensive, Adam says the opportunities in transition to fully organic products as an important ideal for society. This is reflected
in the range of products that are not fully organic, but their environmentally
based reducing harmful and toxic substances from the living and work environments where the products are eventually used. The suppliers are therefore vital for
the business model of the company. Supplies are also vital for the company as one
of the unique value propositions of the company is excellent customer service and
timely delivery. To ensure this business model is intact, the suppliers of the
company of vital and good relations with these organisations allow for the Plant
Doctor to be successful. As the trend for more healthy products continues, the
transition from environmentally friendly products to fully organic products will
continue. The company is very attuned to changes in market demand for environmental products that align with the continued trend towards healthy people,
plants and animals.

Reporting Impact of the Plant Doctor Focus on Health and Well-Being

The main way that Plant Doctor measures impact is through testimonials and feedback from customers. The value proposition of health and well-being has resonated with the customers, and the diverse and increasing range of natural-based and organic products offered exemplifies a positive impact in the community they serve. Also, the awards that Plant Doctor received are a testament to the impact and success of the business. In 2019, Plant Doctor was selected as Best Family Business for August. Also in 2020, Plant Doctor received another award from the Gold Coast Business Awards for Best Family Business for the year, followed in May 2022 as Business of the Month for the category of Manufacturing (shown in Fig. 4).

Troy (Production and Techincal) and Jami (Corporate Manager) from the team at Plant Doctor said, 'Our good old fashioned service assists us with being able to respond to customer's needs, we try to have open avenues of contact for our customers to have direct access to us through, a manned phone line, social media and a well watched emails serviced by staff who care and want to help find the best solution for people making contact with us. Some days during COVID-19 lockdowns the phoneline was the only access some of our customers had to a conversation out of their homes, especially some of our elderly customers, and it was great to be the friendly voice of light to a dark time'.

Fig. 4.   Current Employees of Plant Doctor Receive Awards.

Plant Doctor believes healthy living and eating is a right. They find an open mind is needed to fulfil their clients diverse needs. One the one hand their clients want to control of their food chain by growing food at home whereas others want supplements to top up their food supply with missing key nutrition or elements. Keeping active in online spaces where their customers interact with each other allows Plant Doctor to keep ahead of the competition and gives insight into gaps in the market to focus their product development and innovation. Essentially being a small to medium enterprise gives them the ability to steer the ship in a new direction when required. They claim to listen and more importantly they claim to listen:

> At Plant Doctor we recognise that not all people can afford to go organic or renewable at every part of their life, but may be able to introduce it in smaller areas, as our suppliers have more products available we are working towards implementing and updating our products to include healthier and environmentally friendlier options at an affordable price. These changes are small but do have impacts beyond our own space, we all need to start somewhere.
>
> (Troy Edge, 2023)

The Plant Doctor has a philosophical position on the transition to deep sustainability. They believe most people, for example, can't drive an electric car right now or quit burning coal for electricity, but people can think about transition and business can assist in the transition. Companies like Plant Doctor can think of transition products and start to source products and services from like-minded sustainable-oriented businesses. Plant Doctor has renewable energy sources and extensive recycling. All their sites have solar power or purchase from renewable energy to reduce their need for fossil fuel electricity and assist with air pollution wherever possible. Plant Doctor utilised recycled cardboard and non-virgin plastics for packaging. They also have separated waste streams and have access to a farm where they dispose of any excess fertiliser to pasture, ensuring the business has all its waste recycled or utilised as much as possible before landfill is used as an option. As the Plant Doctor develops, they will identify more places to improve and adopt changes.

When the Plant Doctor first 'discovered' the SDGs, they didn't realise how much their business was already aligned with the SDGs. The family business did not need to change the business model and noted that having an alignment with the SDGs is just good business practice. The Plant Doctor has a natural desire to have a sustainable business, in an attempt to leave our world a better place and not just to pursue SDG#3 but to contribute to all SDGs.

Challenges of Working With SDG#3 Health and Well-Being

Plant Doctor faces several challenges. These challenges can impact its operations, growth and overall success. The first major challenge is the seasonal nature of the horticultural industry. The demand for plant care services is seasonal, with peak periods during spring and summer. Managing workload fluctuations and maintaining consistent revenue throughout the year is offset by other elements of the business and also providing online services so local geography is less of an issue. A growing population also allows for increased demand for products, and this allows other plant care professionals an opportunity to become established. Focusing on the value proposition of health and well-being is a way to overcome this competition and retain customers. As part of this, Plant Doctor stays up to date with the latest horticultural practices and plant health trends, but this requires continuous learning and development.

Another challenge is educating customers about the importance of the health and well-being dimensions of the products they purchase. Organic products and general healthcare products tend to be more expensive, and thus, educating potential customers on the value perception of such products is a challenge. Marketing is important in establishing a strong brand presence to create and reach their target audience in a competitive market.

Plant Doctor is also scaling up operations, and this can be a challenge. As the business grows, maintaining quality standards while scaling operations to meet demand can be challenging, particularly in terms of hiring and training skilled staff. Also during this time-building and maintaining positive relationships with clients and stakeholders, understanding their needs and delivering satisfactory results are critical for long-term success. Training new staff is vital.

Lastly, the family business prides itself on customer satisfaction and displays customer reviews throughout its online presence. Plant Doctor has a continual challenge of ensuring a high level of customer satisfaction. Managing issues effectively is crucial for maintaining a positive reputation. To overcome these challenges, the Plant Doctor business needs a strategic approach to keep SDG#3 Health and Well-Being as a central value proposition if it wants to contribute to SDG#3.

Business and Greater Good

The market for organic products is steadily increasing in Australia and internationally. In Australia, the increase in demand for organic products has increased dramatically. In 2022, 56% of Australian shoppers have purchased organic in the last year, and of those people, 62% of shoppers cited personal health as a motivator for their initial organic purchase. There has been a 38% growth in organic certified operators between 2011 and 2022 (Ausorganic, 2023).

Plant Doctor has been a pioneer in health and well-being in the region and will continue to provide natural and organic products for people plants and animals. The family business contributes to the greater good through its value proposition. The rising consumer demand for organic products will see an increase in demand for Plant Doctor's 'normal' business activities, and thus, there will be greater environmental benefits arising from their business activities.

What Next for Plant Doctor and SDG#3?

The future development on the cards for Plant Doctor and associated companies in the group includes identifying new markets in horticultural products that are organic or organic-based. The capacity of the company to pivot to producing new products is high as a result of developing in-house packaging and labelling facilities as well as warehouse capacity for storage and dispatch. Expanding the range of products will overcome some of the challenges outlined above like seasonality and also price competitiveness. Plant Doctor and associated companies also have learnt from the COVID-19 pandemic and have strengthened relations with suppliers of products. In the future, Plant Doctor and the group will continue to place health and well-being as a core element of the business model and by doing so can advance the goal of SDG#3.

References

Australian Organic. (2023). *Organic produce consumption surges since COVID-19.* https://austorganic.com/organic-produce-consumption-surges-since-covid-19/. Accessed on August 20, 2023.

Plant Doctor. (2023). *Products and services offered by Plant Doctor.* https://www. plantdoctor.com.au/. Accessed on August 20, 2023.

Index

Printed and bound by CPI Group (UK) Ltd, Croydon, CR0 4YY

12/12/2023

08206976-0001